To Paul,
 for the future!

   Peter.

Essays and Studies 1987

The English Association

The object of the English Association is to promote understanding and appreciation of the English language and its literature.

The Association is an international organization with branches at home and overseas. Its activities include sponsoring a number of publications and organizing annual sixth-form conferences.

Publications

The Year's Work in English Studies. An annual bibliographical survey of scholarly books and articles on English, American and Commonwealth Literature and Language. Published by John Murray (USA: Humanities Press).

Essays and Studies. An annual anthology of essays usually on a wide range of subjects from the medieval to the modern. A collector is nominated every year by the Association. Published by John Murray (USA: Humanities Press).

English. The journal of the Association, *English* is published three times a year by the Oxford University Press.

The Presidential Address. The Presidential Address, usually on a literary or linguistic subject, is published annually.

News-Letter. A *News-Letter* is issued three times a year giving information about forthcoming publications, conferences, and other activities.

Occasional Publications. The Association has published or sponsored many occasional works including *A Guide to Degree Courses in English* (Sixth Edition 1982), *English Grammar For Today*, *English Short Stories of Today*, *Poems of Today*, and many pamphlets.

Membership

There are three categories of membership. Full members receive copies of *The Year's Work in English Studies*, *Essays and Studies*, *English* (3 issues), three *News-Letters* and the Presidential Address.

Ordinary Members receive *English* (3 issues), three *News-Letters* and the Presidential Address.

Member Schools receive two copies of each issue of *English*, one copy of *Essays and Studies* (optional), three *News-Letters* and the Presidential Address. Schools Membership also offers preferential booking for Sixth Form Conference places.

For further details write to The Secretary, The English Association, 1 Priory Gardens, London W4 1TT.

Essays and Studies 1987

ENGLISH AND CULTURAL STUDIES

Broadening the Context

Edited by
MICHAEL GREEN
in association with
RICHARD HOGGART

for the English Association

JOHN MURRAY, LONDON
HUMANITIES PRESS, ATLANTIC HIGHLANDS, N.J.

ESSAYS AND STUDIES 1987
IS VOLUME FORTY IN THE NEW SERIES
OF ESSAYS AND STUDIES COLLECTED ON BEHALF OF
THE ENGLISH ASSOCIATION

© The English Association 1987

First published 1987
by John Murray (Publishers) Ltd
50 Albemarle Street, London W1X 4BD

All rights reserved
Unauthorized duplication contravenes applicable laws

Typeset by Fakenham Photosetting Ltd, Fakenham, Norfolk
Printed and bound in Great Britain at
The Bath Press, Avon

British Library Cataloguing in Publication Data

Essays and studies.
1. English literature—History and
criticism—Periodicals
820.9   PR1
ISBN 0–7195–4369–X
ISBN 0–7195–4402–5 Pbk

First published 1987 in the United States of America by
HUMANITIES PRESS INTERNATIONAL, INC.
Atlantic Highlands, NJ   07716

The Library of Congress has cataloged this serial
publication as follows:

Essays and studies (London, England: 1950)
Essays and studies: being volume 40 of the new series of essays
and studies collected for the English Association—1950-
—London: J. Murray, [1950-
v.: ill.; 22 cm.
Annual.
ISSN 0071–1357 = Essays and Studies

Title varies slightly.
Vols. for 1950–1981 called also new ser., v. 3–v. 34.
Continues: English studies (London, England)

1. English literature—History and criticism.   2. English philology—Collections.   I. English Association.   II. Title.   III. Title: Essays & studies.
PR13.E4   820.4   36–8431
AACR 2   MARC-S

Library of Congress [8509r85]rev5

ISBN 0–391–03551–7

Contents

INTRODUCTION: POINTS OF DEPARTURE—'NEW'
SUBJECTS AND 'OLD' 1
Michael Green

WHY BRECHT, OR, IS THERE ENGLISH AFTER
CULTURAL STUDIES? 20
Peter Brooker

TRAVESTIES OF DICKENS 32
Paul Hoggart

THE MYSTIQUE OF THE BACHELOR GENTLEMAN
IN LATE VICTORIAN MASCULINE ROMANCE 45
Michael Skovmand

'GREAT EXPECTATIONS': MASCULINITY AND
MODERNITY 60
Carolyn Brown

DIFFERENT STARTING-POINTS: A VIEW OF
TEACHING 'ENGLISH ETC' FROM FURTHER
EDUCATION 75
Dee Edwards, David Maund, John Maynard

DAMNING THE TIDES: THE NEW ENGLISH AND
THE REVIEWERS 91
Tony Davies

FEAR OF THE HAPPY ENDING: 'THE COLOR
PURPLE', READING AND RACISM 103
Alison Light

ENGLISH TEACHING AND MEDIA EDUCATION:
CULTURE AND THE CURRICULUM 118
David Lusted

Notes on editors and contributors 129

Introduction: Points of Departure—'New' Subjects and 'Old'

MICHAEL GREEN

When Richard Hoggart was invited to edit this collection he suggested that the essays might in different ways discuss or exhibit the impact of cultural studies on the work of English departments.

It's now more than twenty years since a Centre for Contemporary Cultural Studies was formed as a small postgraduate unit of the English department at Birmingham University. Since then cultural studies has emerged—in quite various forms and places—alongside a cluster of new curriculum developments in the humanities. In one way what has happened in cultural studies (first in Britain, then in other parts of the world) is part of the spread of 'theoretical work' which has a global significance, if at times in some problematical, perhaps too readily 'multi-national' forms. In another way, cultural studies disconcerts the boundaries of 'the humanities' (as well as of 'high culture') because of its exchanges with social history, anthropology and sociology: it is not a discipline committed above all to the text. Pragmatically, in England, cultural studies is one of those strong, but awkward, minority presences in school and degree work. It has links with film studies, media studies and communications studies; with feminist work in various disciplines and, less commonly in Britain, in 'women's studies' as such; and with the contested work being done in multi-cultural and anti-racist education.

This then is a story of educational, political and social developments in Britain since the 1960s, and it displays the distinctive marks of the 'English case'. The present situation is clearly highly contradictory. Maps of educational knowledge have been notably redrawn. Forms of teaching have changed in response to student and staff pressures. Secondary curricula can be taught of an intellectual richness and interdisciplinary weight that are very welcome. At the same time the whole state educational system is disorganized and in retrenchment combined with low morale. The energy of policymakers is given to an ambitious 'new vocationalism' for 16 to 19 year olds, and to tighter 'management' priorities. There is talk of a centralized national curriculum in which the understanding of synecdoche in English may be important. Yet on the desk sit the impressive first two issues of *News from Nowhere*, published by Oxford English Ltd as 'the Journal of the Oxford English Faculty Opposition'. Two or three of the essays in this book tell an English story which might still be significant elsewhere—just as accounts of such developments in the States, Europe or Australia are from England hard to come by, though very much wanted.

Meanwhile the shifts in 'English' are displayed when this book appears in the longstanding *Essays and Studies* series from the English Association, with its own British and Commonwealth role in curriculum change in the past.

For it was this Association which in the early years of the century had to battle to establish a timetable place for a new, dubious and excessively 'contemporary' subject (!), perhaps for those who 'could not cope with' the Classics; which took key positions on the influential Newbolt Committee before its 1921 *Report on the Teaching of English*; and which by the 1930s had achieved both its primary goal of instigating the expansion of English in schools and the 'assured position it now held'. So successful was its educational campaigning that its later turn to an annual collection of scholarly essays in literary history depended on a belief (on the face of it, a correct one) that the place of English in school curricula was permanently secure.[1] What by a post-war generation was then inherited as a 'natural' or traditional or obvious subject, with customary ways and procedures unruffled by Cold War circumstances, was in truth of disputed and quite recent origin. Current arguments about the purposes and practices of English, the exclamations of 'crisis' and panic denial, go straight back to much earlier debates about the subject. They also take up quite new issues: these arise both from the theoretical work of the 1970s, and from the social relations and cultural forms (spectacularly more visible since the 1960s), the hopes and demands of new social groupings, which cultural studies had tried to address.

This volume is framed in different ways then: by a greater degree of dialogue, at least in the lower ranks, between the apparently 'old' discipline of English and lines of work in cultural studies; by the nevertheless extreme disparity in their institutional position (English often compulsory, always popular, on a huge scale in schools, further and higher education—media studies becoming more active in schools—cultural studies an outcrop in a very few places); and by a social and political situation in which further extensive educational changes seem (in wildly differing versions) urgently desirable. These changes will on the face of it either be by way of confirming and entrenching the 'new settlement' of Labour and Conservative administrations in the last ten years, or by a strenuous campaign to make education more challenging, more satisfying and more democratic—not just in forms of provision and access, but *inside the subject groupings* of the curriculum.[2]

It is therefore hoped that the essays in this short collection will do three things at this particular time, as one small part of a more extensive, urgent and (despite the recent contraction) inspiring movement of re-formation. One, they contain various thoughts upon the respective states of English, media and cultural studies, on the ways in which they question and energize each other. Though situations differ between educational sectors and between this and other countries, there is throughout an effort to think through a new kind of humanities teaching and research which will be more adequate to human needs, the needs of all human beings rather than a few, in current circumstances. Two, we wanted there to be a sense of disparate teaching situations and problems: we wished if possible to include here work touching on all levels of education (primary schooling is a major omission), besides registering how cultural studies became important to the more unified teaching of foreign languages and literatures. A movement towards cultural studies is in fact highly developed internationally, often with more support and less selfconsciousness, with less fear of the present or the future, than in Britain. Three, some of the essays locate themes and ideas from various discourses, including narrative fiction, in ways not characterisic of 'text/context' or 'literature and society' approaches. In them the object of attention is neither the 'literary' text nor such texts 'and theory'. Instead the concern is with cultural forms: with effects and relationships of power and subordination within and between them, with the larger cultural field in which their place is constructed. Dickens, masculinity, and the filiations between 'serious' and 'popular' cultural forms are all looked at from more than one direction. We would like to have included more writing on English and cultural studies in what an inadequate and misleadingly equalizing adjective calls a multi-racial Britain; nevertheless for English, media or cultural studies *The Color Purple*, whose ability to uplift and disturb is considered here, seems one good place of departure.

This short introduction annotates some relevant developments. To begin with there is a review of the 'break' of cultural studies inside and to an extent away from English. Then a look at some of the mutations in English as a subject is higher and in secondary/further education; and at the development of cultural studies in close contact but no substantial alignment with the parallel growth of media and communications studies. Last, there is a comment on the current situation in such work: on the potentialities of this moment in education, on the need for ways of working which are intellectually satisfying for staff and students but with which they can also cope. Some of the ambitions for this work are rightly very great: how can what they offer be delivered?

Both *The Uses of Literacy* (1957) and *The Long Revolution* (1961), though grounded in literary criticism, pushed the recently drawn boundaries of English departments in ways not readily accommodated.[3] *The Long Revolution* used examples from the 1840s to illustrate the selectivity of 'tradition', to show that what could later be presented as an a-historical canon of aesthetic distinction involved suppressions of the past and choices in the present; and it argued that cultural forms were always more various than dominant versions of 'Culture' were prepared to allow. It drew on educational history, on developments in the English language, and on 'mass' media forms to offer an analysis of the 1960s and to outline the bases of an unfolding (indeed almost inevitable—a view sharply rejected in Williams's later work) democratic cultural revolution. *The Uses of Literacy*, also 'concerned with cultural change', disrupted the advertised promises of a post-war affluence in which class differences would be eroded, or vanish. It looked at many aspects of working class life, including magazines and comics but also proverbs, speech patterns and common sense, to try to find out how 'mass' media, along with other forces, would 'connect with commonly accepted attitudes, how they are altering those attitudes, and how they are meeting resistance' (ch. 1). The cultural forms of such resistance, especially in youth subcultures (Willis's *Learning to Labour*, Hebdige's *Subculture, Resistance Through Rituals* by Hall and others) became the main concern of early work at the Birmingham Centre.

These were studies of the cultural forms *of the present*, driven by political judgements about social change and not by the wish to 'appreciate'—though certainly in part to celebrate. In various ways they broke the limits of a literary canon made to seem 'completed' by the modernism of the '20s with its now 'postmodern' contemporary world. Similarly they went beyond 'literary' procedures around the detailed reading of particular texts of high 'aesthetic' value. The central effort was to judge the determinants and directions of postwar culture: for instance, the value of those 'saved by and locked within' subcultural groupings, in Angela McRobbie's phrase.

In France, Barthes and others were making similar moves away from the canon of French language and literature towards cinema, advertising and popular culture (wrestling, the Tour de France), provoking the same mixture of extensive interest and energetic opposition. In Barthes's work the hoped-for 'science' of semiology, the study of signs (and his attachment to epigram, aphorism and pun, foreign to English moral thought) displaced the English attention to everyday life and speech forms on the one hand and to institutional changes on the other. Yet Barthes also offered through his theory of myth a new account of ideology, which along with other Marxist concepts and a view of contemporary society as fissured by divisions, conflicts and struggle rather than being (or becoming) a 'whole way of life' was soon to dominate British analyses.[4] In both countries the main interest was in the work done through the construction and exchange of meanings—in the media, in style, in signifying activities of many kinds—in a society displaying unequally spectacular changes, new social groupings, and a relentless reproduction of divisions and inequalities.

Looking back, it may have been a diversion (prompted by the historical procedures of higher education and its sanctioned academic knowledge forms) to promote such work as ' interdisciplinary'. Using that term tended to freeze the various 'disciplines' into their customary places in the academic division of labour. Seeking to establish the basis for a new kind of enterprise, it reified the English, History, Sociology and so on which it sought to transcend. It looks to have been a wrong-footed claim. Partly, because the various disciplines—first Sociology, then much later English (quite apart from the 'absent' challenge of Marxist thought)—were quickly seen to be more plural, more fractured, more contradictory, than had appeared. Also, because in any case as Barthes observed later

> interdisciplinary work ... begins *effectively* when the solidarity of the old disciplines breaks down ... to the benefit of a new object and a new language, neither of which is in the domains of those branches of knowledge that one calmly sought to confront.[5]

Yet the *institutional* forms of disciplines, in the impoverishment of the 1980s, are scowlingly entrenched, regardless of their intellectual claims. Work in cultural studies for instance can be *variously* classified, or *not* classified *at all* in the 'cost groupings' of higher education management; while in secondary and further English teaching it is the examination boards, with their disparate syllabuses and 'modes' which will in practice allow or forbid new forms of work— as in one board's recent (perhaps poignant) stipulation that student work in English must still show 'a discernible relation to a text'.

The other matter for surprise, looking back to the point of departure from English of cultural studies, is that so little was done about language. The situation of language studies is puzzling. The division in English departments of English 'language and literature', with its practical implication, often, of literacy for all and literature for a few, seems to have divided off from literary studies both historical research into language and the range of modern linguistics—where much work is very interesting in detail yet persistently formal and without much drawing out of social and cultural implications. By contrast in cultural studies there have been few particular analyses of language at all: a main line of thought has been the treacherous pursuit of culture itself as 'structured like a language', only sometimes qualified by references to work by Labov or by Voloshinov/ Bakhtin which understands linguistic shifts as social struggle and conflict in language.[6] Language remains a main area where cultural studies and English might come together but which both recurrently neglect.[7]

It is hard to judge how necessary were the fraught procedures of academic separation. There were people who saw cultural studies work as a betrayal of moral and literary value ('*Middlemarch* is *better than* soap opera', as though that were the issue), or its development of theroretical readings as anathema. Conversely there was a willingness in cultural studies too readily to ignore or repress the memory of novels, plays and paintings or of the social relations of museums, bookshops and theatres. There was a period when (despite Williams's warnings) 'bourgeois culture' was simply ignored.[8] This cannot be the case now. There is a considerably sharper interest in dominant cultural forms and institutions: partly because of a stronger sense of the field of cultural politics—of women's writings and other forms of production, of community arts, of the range of alternative practices and independent production in theatre, cinema and video; partly through respect for the Greater London Council work on cultural industries and on a London cultural policy just before the Council's abolition; and also through an appreciation of the force of American and British campaigns for cultural democracy and for a charter of cultural rights.[9] Given, however, the founding of cultural studies in disjunction from English, their incomplete and still qualified independence, what have been some of the significant changes since the tense relations between the two of the early 1970s?

In English (though this has happened in thoroughly uneven ways and to an inconsistent degree) four developments seem to stand out. The first is the partial deconstruction of the subject itself: both of the canon which it constructs and reproduces and of the exclusive priority given to a sensitive liberal response to particular texts. Ten years ago it looked as though a genial critical pluralism would be stabilized, in which new social movements could be inscribed and accommodated (here a Marxist, there a feminist, nowhere as yet any sense of imperialism or of 'race'): their attentions still mainly directed towards the received textual corpus. Now, the canon is seen to have excluded most writing by women, much contemporary writing and narrative and fictional work in 'new' media, and a huge area dismissed as 'popular culture'. Work has been done on the links between the subject of English and a particular construction of English-ness: attention drawn to the 'national' language and literature in which conflicts and social differences are subordinated to the 'progress' of a unified, coherent whole; and to a sense of 'heritage', part founded in the literary, which is both recent and Imperial, a nationhood looking persistently backwards, occluding its boundaries from larger metropolis-periphery and first world-third world relations.[10] In particular, we now know much more about the disputed foundations of the discipline and, inside its development, about the ways in which its coherence and social purpose have had *always* to be defined and redefined in altered circumstances.[11] This is a revealing history of state education and of the groups who come to shape its development; and it quite permanently alters, in conjunction with the other new considerations, the taken-for-granted status of English as a subject.

Second, and despite the still recurring opposition to the fantasized dangers of 'theories', there is a remarkable adjustment, especially in the United States, to the realization that 'knowledge creates its object'. Althusser's phrase is too neat and it discourages questions about *how* knowledge comes to be as it is, what forces shape *it*. Yet it does concisely insist that decisions about what should be studies and in what ways cannot be secondary or marginal to the empirical innocence of intuitive responses to what is 'on the page'. He urges that we should make visible and accessible what questions are being asked, what priorities established, what kind of work is taking place. Following the publication of so much theoretical work, changes in expectations (even more in what is expected from students) have indeed been very great. Work informed by a range of theory may still, however, typically turn its attention to the canonical text. It could even be that the close reading of theoretical texts may replace and be more attractive than the reading of the literature of the canon. Yet much of this work has obviously transformed the range and clarity of questions which may be asked. I.A. Richards has been described as refusing

> elements of collusion (in a) tradition of appreciation: the informed, assured and familiarized discourse of people talking among themselves about works which from a shared social position they had been privileged to know

—while it would now be agreed that a few years later Leavis and others were also challenging and broadening the class composition of literary discussion.[12] In the same way the attempt at theoretical clarification has been one of the modes in which new social groups have been able to speak in higher education, quite apart from the new interests, above all in subjectivity and in forms of pleasure, which this work has instigated.

Third, there is a pronounced movement (perhaps stronger in secondary and further than in higher education) towards diversifying the corpus of texts to be studied. Women's writings across all known genres and outside them begin to occupy a central place which is still denied to women *teachers* towards the 'higher' educational echelons. Interest is not turning away from 'literature' but is certainly engaged by writings more broadly defined, by the understanding of many kinds of signification and forms of representation as social and historical forms of consciousness. The move need not suspend questions of 'aesthetic' or social value, but it refuses to grant them any privileged position in particular texts. Terry Eagleton calls for the study of rhetoric. Raymond Williams defines cultural materialism as

> the analysis of all forms of signification, including quite centrally writing, within the actual means and conditions of their production[13]

even if 'quite centrally' remains to be argued about. This may be a slow recovering of what can now be understood to have once been a much fuller definition of literature, culture and criticism.[14] So a useful recent anthology for 'A' level presents a varied collection which might 'motivate a wide range of purposeful language activities' and includes 'period' studies and texts which articulate documentary, local, oral and black perspectives.[15]

Fourth, these redefinitions of what English can be take on a sustained organizational form. In publishing, the *New Accents* series stands out. There has been an influential series of conferences: in the sociology of literature at Essex University (and now in the annual series of cross-cultural conferences there) organized around particular years in literary production and the conjunctures of which they are part; in literary theory at the University of Southampton; at some of the conferences and day schools organized through the National Association of Teachers of English. *The English Magazine* from the Inner London Education Authority English Centre has consistently produced outstandingly lucid and well-informed work across English, media and cultural studies, paying attention to problems of teaching and learning.[16] LTP (Literature, Teaching, Politics), a network of groups with a regular journal and annual conference, has debated these developments, their teaching implications, and their connection with cultural discussion and production outside education itself.[17] In all these ways the character and aims of 'English' are thus going through extensive debate and transformation across a variety of teaching sites.

In contrast cultural studies has never become fully a 'subject' at all: perhaps few would have wished it to be such. On one reading cultural studies exists only as a precariously won space in which many kinds of critical work, unvalued by other subjects or expelled from them, can take place. For the most part cultural studies has been found in the margins of other subjects, and in the spaces between them: at times a critique of absences in various disciplines, at others a meeting-point, across Faculties, which is not fully Humanities (because locating the cultural in the development of the social formation) yet rather less Social Science (because wanting to analyse and interpret closely the making and taking of meaning). It can arise in productive tension with other activities—at the edges of work in English or History or Sociology, or in degrees whose origins, unity and rationale still bear the marks of particular subject formations. Or, less visibly, cultural studies work is being constructed in practice-based teaching (music, drama, photography, art and design) as a more coherent body of work to replace the 'complementary' or 'general' studies mixed bag. Perhaps the stablest opportunity for cultural studies work to develop, here and in Europe, has been in departments of foreign languages and literatures where the chance is welcomed to look beyond the classic text, to bring together work in literature, history and social studies, to think about cultural forms and contemporary society outside the confining frame of 'literature and its background'.[18] There is almost no example of fully-fledged cultural studies 'as such': no such space in school curricula, in higher education a yoking of cultural studies to other work in a more mixed enterprise—either with traditional humanities subjects, or in the new formations of media and communication studies.

It seems worth asking why this should be so. The question is inextricably one of intellectual aims (what *is* the object of analysis in cultural studies?) and of institutional strategy (how in general *should* humanities curricula be changed?). Has cultural studies been restricted by contraction and by the priorities of curriculum management or was it always a reluctant candidate for disciplinary promotion? What distinctive space should cultural studies occupy? Does it mark out a specific ground in a coherent way; or is it better understood as a set of concerns and questions to be put and developed across all subjects, assuming that one of those is now to be media studies?

The history of cultural studies has been restless and at times confusing. It is rewarding to understand the momentum of developments, much harder to define, especially in teaching terms, an accessible and coherent object of study. We know that cultural studies in Britain began in adult education; that it was an attempt to think about post-war changes in which questions to do with culture and signification and forms of consciousness were of central social and political significance; that it worked in an area where the work of Leavis and other literary critics seemed to have stopped short and Marxism, as then understood, scarcely to have begun. We can look back on the difficult encounter between close readings of cultural forms (advertisements, newspapers, style and speech in youth subcultures) and the take-up, at great speed, of Marxist and other forms of social theory.[19] Feminism served notice upon the gender-blindness and male-centred preoccupations of the work undertaken.[20] Now anti-racist imperatives re-question what is done in other ways. This is a narrative of violently compressed intellectual movement: at best responding to changes in the society of which the 'subject' forms part, at worst too mobile and condensed to be coped with, especially in a way that could be learnt or taught.

Two of the ways in which the coherence of cultural studies has been argued are extremely ambitious. It may be proposed that the different inflections of the term culture and of other concepts which should be set against its dangerous slide and spread (ideology, hegemony) signal a theoretical history in which no object of study may be straightforwardly acknowledged: in which cultural studies draws consistent attention to the complexity of the analysis of meanings, but also to the diverse and even contradictory significance of the 'cultural' sphere itself (we can speak of cultural *practice* yet also of cultural *reproduction*) in a larger account of societies and of social change.[21] Or, that cultural forms are a ground of constant transformation may be emphasized by looking at a 'circuit', including conditions of production, and the social relations of reading or 'consumption' or use, through which cultural practices pass, as a set of stages each with its own specificity inside a more complex process.[22] Both these formulations underestimate or even mask ways in which cultural studies projects have been political interventions, often bitterly contested, inside subjects unwilling to acknowledge that cultures and cultural forms may be where dissatisfactions and aspirations, social criticisms, are spoken: 'the study of culture always has a political dimension, the suppression of which is also, precisely, political'.[23]

A programme of work in cultural studies in ideal form will want to move across three areas, though in ways that may diverge in their starting-points and theoretical concerns. There will be some sense, first, perhaps in an historically informed analysis or through theoretical accounts, but always in other everyday ways too, of what a society is like. This will increasingly include analysis of how national, regional and local boundaries and identities are constructed, of international and cross-national movements which they mask. This work has a meeting-point with sociology in its concern with power and the inflections of class, gender, 'racial' and other divisions: it differs from sociology in its primary emphasis on meanings. It will want to look at views of the world which come to be dominant, to seem taken for granted, natural or obvious, whether in formal public statements or in common sense: so it will engage with analyses which think about this domination in varied ways through concepts that cannot be straightforwardly aligned with each other—ideology, hegemony, power, discourse, reproduction.[24] In the last few years in fact work around these terms has almost displaced the original starting-point which was interested in how social groupings and divisions are 'culturally' formed, made sense of, inhabited, transformed.

This necessary presence of theories of power and meaning is clearly one of the ways in which cultural forms are, second, not straightforwardly available to be studied. To talk about cultural forms (without wanting to subsume them as moments of ideology or as instances of discourse, though both discussions are important) is to look at ways of making sense which may take the *form* of a text but can only *provisionally* be *treated* as such—in sharp distinction to traditional readings of the text in English. Meanings, it may be said, are not the property of forms in themselves, of objects: they exist in the relations and in the differences between themselves and other forms (the documentary form is assertively *not* 'entertainment'—*The Sun* proclaims that it is other than the *Daily Mirror* or *The Guardian*); and in the relations between the forms and their users. So all kinds of questions may be pursued about the historical conditions or production mediations which lead to a form being as it is. Much can be said of a range of forms available at a given moment, and so of the construction of a field of cultural difference which marks out diverse senses of identity, of pleasure, of individuality and 'choice'. And perhaps the richest work lies in studying users' perceptions, meanings in use and meanings in practice, the subjectivities for which the form itself is the occasion. The text or form in itself has only a provisional or momentary existence for analysis; and even in that moment, as feminist re-readings of classic texts have so strikingly shown, our own perceptions and priorities are, rightly, part of what we analyse.

This in turn means that cultural studies will want to know about particular groups of people and their attitudes, values, stances; about the uses they make of particular forms, at what might be called their cultural strategies. To this end the major contributions have been from various kinds of 'ethnographies' including participant observation, semi-structured and informal taped interviews, and so forth. Recently Dave Morley has considerably complicated such accounts, arguing that reading is

> a question of how social position plus particular discourse posi-

tions produce specific readings: readings which are structured because the structure of access to different discourses is determined by social position.[25]

More generally then cultural studies aims not to produce interpretations of texts but to look at what forms seem to be for: what space do they occupy, how are they used, what sense do they make and for whom? These questions require us to know something about the historical circumstances in which particular forms have come to be so and not otherwise, though still in change; and something about the kinds of significance they possess, the work they do, the knowledge or hope or imaginary resolution they afford for those by whom the forms are taken up. Many examples of this kind of work can now be cited: on black music and white teenagers, on Kung Fu films and their audiences, on romance fiction and women readers.[26]

In all this there are substantial points of connection with other related subjects. Cultural studies shares with English an interest in the close analysis of cultural forms, particularly those which for various reasons seem striking and significant to contemporary circumstances. They depart from some (but not all) forms of English in looking beyond the literary text, as they depart from media studies in looking beyond print and broadcast media—but then the disciplinary division of literary and 'new' media *should* have been redundant by the 1930s, as it was for Walter Benjamin. They share with some kinds of communications studies (not those which are only indefinitely pluralist, or concerned with a transparent or vocationally directed conflict-free communicative competence) an intention to locate cultural forms or communications among uneven forms of power in society and the unequal exchange of meaning. All these bodies of work will have something to say of readers and readings, or audiences, or what is called consumption in an influential version of media studies (looking at production, text, consumption as three moments).[27] If this account of changes in English and of the growth of cultural studies is plausible then the issue is no longer one of how they might work together: between them, and in their mutual connections with media or communication studies, there are points of convergence already.

On the question of the institutional drawing of curricula boundaries, it seems unlikely that cultural studies will become in itself a subject, except in rare cases. It will more probably become a way of framing an agenda, a series of questions and approaches, a political and intellectual framework, inside and alongside the curriculum subjects: the central humanities subjects of English or History; performance- and practice-based subjects whether in drama, music or visual areas; the new curricula in media studies and in communications. David Lusted has argued that cultural studies is not a subject but could become a basis upon which the humanities are recast and their subjects become regrouped.[28] English in its broadest definition, extending to media of all kinds but also to the intellectual issues evolving in media, communications and cultural analysis, seems sure to remain of pivotal importance in that formation.

What might concern us more is whether, and for whom, this kind of work is *feasible*: not just if all the various debates in the relevant areas are attended to, but if on any level the aims are to be carried through. Is the agenda impossibly large and so (ironically) extremely academic? Can it be carried through in ways which are satisfying yet also manageable? Does it require an unusually confident willingness to cross social and disciplinary boundaries, to risk a considerable intellectual, emotional and political stake; can it take place outside the now vanishing (in Britain) space of a funded doctoral thesis?

These questions cannot be answered here and now. Time is needed to find ways of working whose aims can be achieved. Peter Widdowson commented pertinently in 1980 that a greater self-consciousness about theory and method may allow

> little or no operational space to those ... who are not ... concerned with the production of theory, but who wish to understand and occupy the new spaces ... and who are teaching 'Literature' with deep dissatisfaction ... This predicament results in teachers/critics abandoning the field ... either by actually leaving it for other more 'progressive' studies ('cultural' and 'communications' studies, for example) ... or by developing an intellectual schizophrenia.[29]

We could anticipate three mutually supporting ways in which feasible bodies of work, in learning, teaching and research, might be encouraged.

One of these is precisely those efforts being made in various institutional contexts to define a set of endeavours in which aims may be accomplished without 'impossible' ambitions. No longer is it what is to be done but what are ways of carrying it through, with what problems, in different educational sectors. Tony Bennett's demanding article on the problems of constructing the Open University's Popular Culture course is exemplary in its attention to the implications of marking out an adequate 'teaching object ... assessed strategically in terms of any lines of development it opens up'.[30] Also welcome are the first articles, just appearing, about course programmes in detail: as in Jon Cook's remarkably full and honest essay about the teaching of a course at the University of East Anglia.[31] For all the adjacent curriculum territories, in English, media, cultural and communications studies, it would be good to have more accounts of cases that worked: where students and teachers carried through, altered, improvised a programme to make it enjoyable as well as useful. As we think more about the 'traditional' pleasures of English, with its capacity to attract students in huge numbers to the re-reading of an imaginative text, we might consider how differently constituted are the attractions of work in cultural studies; and which are certainly not to be found in the replacement of a monotonous textual 'appreciation' by a recurrent cultural 'critique'. (Brecht's 'better the bad new things than the good old ones' was almost a premonition of the dominant stances of media and English studies respectively.)

At the same time this is likely to be a more collaborative exercise than in some other subjects, and on principle: not just because the scope of the work requires a variety of contributions (though that is true), or because of an a priori commitment to some of the real gains of 'progressive' teaching methods, recently discussed in far too simple and caricatured a way as though pupil- or teacher-oriented pedagogies were some straightforward binary choice. Rather as we look at different cultural practices we produce an understanding of their varied interests to us as well as to 'audiences' who are somewhere outside us, to be studied. Instead of producing a shared 'reading community', the previous work of English departments, we are likely to become more conscious of contrasted, even opposing perceptions which are deeply rooted in social relations, which are 'in here' as well as 'out there', and about which we may become more exploratory, in productive ways.

How much more will this be true as *and if* students themselves are no longer drawn so disproportionately from the social groups which have historically occupied the higher reaches of state education. It is quite clear in 1987 that the English educational system is working ever more starkly to select and reproduce for social difference. There is an attempt to confine university education in the main to those who can afford it; polytechnics are urged to take higher numbers on lower resources, and to be more strictly vocational; in the severely unequal provision of secondary schooling and of further education an almost iron division is furthered between the academic few and the 'skill' trained many. So cultural studies cannot be a matter only of an agenda, a programme, a set of curriculum objectives but of who is interested and why:

> cultural studies is a reflection of the fact that the culture we study is our own and, because of that, we are responsible for making as well as analysing it. To create the conditions for that reflection in an institution historically devoted to its denial has been the emergent task of our work in cultural studies.[32]

In that respect the immediate situation seems at once more open, more ambiguous yet also more positive than for some time.

It is readily possible, despite the signs of defensive retrenchment in education, to argue for priorities different to those of the 'new vocationalism' and of the countervailing, contracting 'academic' sphere. We can see signs of this in negotiations over GCSE and alternative 'A' level syllabuses, in the belated and partial D.E.S. and local authority recognition of media studies work, in the movement for the study of language and meaning and representation 'across the curriculum'.[33] It is right to argue, not that those new kinds of work can lead to jobs where those jobs do not exist (though there are most certainly jobs in media and cultural industries which in some degree thrive against the recession), but that these studies meet student interest and need; bring out their best talents; engage them in ways both positive and critical with social questions as they are mediated and developed through contemporary forms of representation. Groups which have been marginalized, excluded or relegated by educational institutions, in particular black people of whom so scandalously few are to be seen in 'academic' streams and subjects, will continue to press for their concerns to be developed: the newer kinds of work discussed in this collection offer one appropriate site. Equally, cultural production itself, most obviously for Channel 4 but of many other kinds, has a stake and a voice in the cultural analysis and debate to which these subjects speak. Those working in community arts and regional arts activity are arguing for cultural democracy: looking for cultural policies which will cross the boundaries of education and of other institutional sites, no longer focused on the 'provision' of 'access' to the traditional cultural sphere but on the making and understanding of new forms adequate to a more fully realized contemporary culture.

'Academic' forms are never only such. New dispositions of subject knowledges do matter, and have their consequences. It is possible to be very optimistic about the changes to come.

Notes

[1] See essays in *Essays and Studies* for 1956 and 1983; and the discussion in Brian Doyle, 'English and Englishness: A Cultural History of English Studies in British Higher Education', Ph.D. thesis (CNAA/Thames Polytechnic, 1986).

[2] See the analysis in CCCS Education Group, *Unpopular Education: Schooling and Social Democracy since 1944* (London, 1981) and in Inge Bates *et al.*, *Schooling for the Dole? The New Vocationalism* (London, 1984).

[3] Richard Hoggart, *The Uses of Literacy* (London, 1957); Raymond Williams, *The Long Revolution* (London, 1961).

[4] Roland Barthes, *Mythologies* (London, 1972).

[5] Roland Barthes, 'From Work to Text' in J.V. Harari, ed., *Textual Strategies: Perspectives in Post-Structuralist Criticism* (London, 1979).

[6] See for instance W. Labov, *Language in the Inner City: Studies in the Black English Vernacular* (Oxford, 1972); V. Volosinov, *Marxism and the Philosophy of Language* (New York, 1973); M. Bakhtin, *Rabelais and his World* (Bloomington, 1984).

[7] Useful relevant examples of such work include George Lakoff and Mark Johnson, *Metaphors We Live By* (Chicago, 1980); Roger Fowler *et al.*, *Language and Control* (London, 1979); Gunther Kress, 'Linguistic and Ideological Transformation in Newspaper Reporting' in H. Davis and P. Walton, eds, *Language, Image, Media* (Oxford, 1983).

[8] Raymond Williams, *Culture and Society 1780–1950* (London, 1958).

[9] See Williams's still cogent proposals in his *Communications* (Harmondsworth, 1962 and revised editions). For the GLC see GLC, *The State of the Art or the Art of the State? Strategies for the Cultural Industries in London* (London, 1985) and the free report *Campaign for a Popular Culture*. Early appraisals of the GLC legacy are in Geoff Mulgan and Ken Worpole, *Saturday Night or Sunday Morning? From Arts to Industry—New Forms of Cultural Policy* (London, 1986) and in Sally Townsend and Franco Bianchini, eds, *Common Pursuits: Cultural Politics Beyond the GLC* (London, 1987). On cultural democracy see for instance Another Standard, *Culture and Democracy: The Manifesto* (London, 1986).

[10] See Brian Doyle, 'Against the Tyranny of the Past', *Red Letters*, 10,

1980, pp. 23–33; R. Balibar, *Les Français Fictifs* (Paris, 1974); P. Macherey and E. Balibar, 'Literature as an ideological form', *Oxford Literary Review*, 3, 1 (1978) pp. 4–12; Tony Davies, 'Education, Ideology and Literature', *Red Letters*, 7, pp. 4–15. All these discuss language, literature and the 'national' canon. Raymond Chapman wrote that 'dates arrive, are celebrated and forgotten, while English literature continues its thousand years of development' in his 'Preface' to *Essays and Studies* (1984). On senses of the past and its heritage see Raymond Williams, *The Country and the City* (London, 1973); and Patrick Wright, *On Living in an Old Country: the National Past in Contemporary Britain* (London, 1985). There are useful essays on Englishness in R. Colls and P. Dodd, eds, *Englishness: Politics and Culture 1880–1920* (London 1986) by Brian Doyle ('The Invention of English', pp. 89–115) and by Peter Brooker and Peter Widdowson ('A Literature for England', pp. 116–63).

[11] There are major new interpretations of the history of the subject in two recent and contrasting Ph.D. theses: Brian Doyle, 'English and Englishness' and John Bowen, 'The Subject of "English": Psychology and Pedagogy from Bain to Richards' (University of Birmingham, 1986). Both seem likely to stimulate much discussion on publication in book form.

[12] Raymond Williams, *Politics and Letters* (London, 1979) continues his earlier discussion in *Culture and Society* of Richards's work: for Leavis see Francis Mulhern, *The Moment of 'Scrutiny'* (London, 1979).

[13] Terry Eagleton, *Literary Theory* (Oxford, 1983); Raymond Williams, *Writing in Society* (London, n.d.) p. 10 (from which the remark on Richards is taken, p. 182).

[14] See entries for Literature and Criticism in Raymond Williams, *Keywords* (London, 1976, revised 1983), and the argument of Terry Eagleton, *The Function of Criticism* (London, 1984).

[15] John Brown and David Jackson, eds, *Varieties of Writing* (London, 1984). See also Roy Goddard's 'Beyond the Literary Heritage: Meeting the Needs in English at 16–19', *English in Education* 19, 2 (Summer 1985) pp. 12–22.

[16] The English Centre (Magazine), Sutherland St, London SW1.

[17] For LTP contact Helen Taylor, Humanities, Bristol Polytechnic, Fishponds, Bristol.

[18] See the excellent discussion by Barry Jordan, 'Modern Languages and the Foreign Culture: from Literary to Cultural Studies', *LTP* 5 (1986) pp. 48–66.

[19] See Stuart Hall *et al.*, eds, *Culture, Media, Language* (London, 1980) for an anthology of Birmingham CCS work.

[20] Examples include Angela McRobbie, 'Settling Accounts with Subcultures', *Screen Education* 34 (Spring 1980), pp. 37–49.

[21] For this approach see Stuart Hall, 'Cultural Studies: Two Paradigms', *Media, Culture and Society* 2, 1 (January 1980) pp. 57–72; or his introduction

to *Culture, Media, Language*; or the forthcoming Stuart Hall, *Cultural Studies: An Introduction* (London, 1987). See also Richard Johnson, 'Three Problematics: Elements of a Theory of Working-Class Culture' in J. Clarke *et al.*, ed, *Working Class Culture* (London, 1979) pp. 201–31.

[22] See Richard Johnson, 'What is Cultural Studies Anyway?', Birmingham CCS stencilled paper (1983). But see also Francis Mulhern, 'Notes on Culture and Cultural Struggle', *Screen Education* 34 (Spring 1980) pp. 31–6.

[23] Allon White, 'From Culture to culture: The Disputed Passage', *Cambridge Review* (May 1975) pp. 128–32, an excellent early discussion on problems of evolving cultural studies from 'present English studies'.

[24] The kind of books that would be important here are, for instance: Jorge Larrain, *The Concept of Ideology* (London, 1979) and *Marxism and Ideology* (London, 1983); Antonio Gramsci, *The Prison Notebooks* (London, 1971); Michel Foucault, *Power/Knowledge: Selected Interviews and Other Writings 1972–77* (Brighton, 1980); Diane Macdonell, *Theories of Discourse* (Oxford, 1986); Pierre Bourdieu, *Distinction* (1984).

[25] Dave Morley, *The 'Nationwide' Audience* (London, 1980), p. 134.

[26] See Simon Jones, 'White Youth and Jamaican Popular Music', Ph.D. thesis (University of Birmingham, 1986); Bob Willis, 'Kung Fu films and black British culture' in Michael Green and Charles Jenkins, eds, *Sporting Fictions*, CCS stencilled papers (Birmingham, 1982); Janice A. Radway's in many ways exemplary *Reading the Romance: Women, Patriarchy and Popular Literature* (Chapel Hill, 1984).

[27] Len Masterman, *Teaching the Media* (London, 1985).

[28] David Lusted, 'Media Studies and Media Education' in *Papers from the Bradford Media Education Conference* (Society for Education in Film and Television, London, 1986) and in this volume.

[29] Peter Widdowson, '"Literary Value" and the Reconstruction of Criticism', *Literature and History* 6, 2 (1980), pp. 138–50, p. 145.

[30] Tony Bennett, 'Popular Culture: A "Teaching Object"', *Screen Education* 34 (Spring 1980), pp. 17–29.

[31] Jon Cook, 'Critiques of culture: a course' in David Punter, ed., *Introduction to Contemporary Cultural Studies* (London, 1986) pp. 119–37. All three essays on teaching in Section B of this collection are well worth reading.

[32] Jon Cook, p. 136.

[33] For these debates see the discussions in the newsletter *Initiatives* published by SEFT; the Scottish *Media Education Journal* published by the Association of Media Educators in Scotland; and, regularly, *The English Magazine, English in Education* and many other journals.

Why Brecht, or, Is There English After Cultural Studies?

PETER BROOKER

Half a dozen years ago the talk was all of the crisis in English. Sides were taken and friends and jobs lost and found as the ideology of English was disclosed and deconstructed, or defended. Some preferred the word crisis in inverted commas as if to suggest it was other people's and not their own. Others told us that we are always in crisis and that there was nothing new about this one. I believe that the word describes a self-conscious reappraisal of the history and ideology of the subject, that English in crisis is English in a process of transformation, and that above all, it is English politicized. As I want to suggest later, cultural studies have played a significant and indeed subversive part in this process. For many, the roles of English and cultural studies as one-time parent and offspring have now been turned about. Moreover, the intellectual pull of cultural studies has drawn English more openly into the arena of its near neighbour, cultural politics. This imbrication of politics and the academy, typical of the crisis, has then brought with it a series of questions, quite new in their explicit form to English, and newer still to England, on the political function of intellectuals and the politics of teaching. Indeed these seem to me to comprise the major themes in the many and detailed challenges there have been to literary and educational orthodoxy. These questions have of course attracted a good deal of theoretical attention in themselves, and sometimes but by no means always their discussion has also been channelled through cultural studies. I am less interested here in their precise derivation, however, and less in matters of theory than of strategy : specifically for reconstituting literary studies as a socially useful domain of intellectual work, teaching, and learning.

It is with this question of strategy in mind that I want to refer to Bertolt Brecht. I want to ask 'Why Brecht?' of others, and of myself as someone researching Brecht. In the context of this essay, my own intellectual development can be regarded as symptomatic evidence: undergraduate years in a very new New University caught in the turbulence of the late 1960s, postgraduate work in the fledgling field

IS THERE ENGLISH AFTER CULTURAL STUDIES? 21

of cultural studies, 'English' teaching in a Polytechnic Humanities School, editing the journal *Literature and History*, and 'living' the crisis. Brecht simply confirms the pattern. It is always Brecht, and sometimes it seems only Brecht, who is being wheeled on as the left's cultural *deus ex machina*. Why?

To cite three recent examples. Graham Holderness, in an article on the use of Shakespeare's *Henry V* in boosting a pro-war mentality in the 1940s, finds signs of a Brechtian 'alienation device' which redeems the text's contradictions and self-criticism in the face of a later ideological use which represses these features. Tony Bennett, in an article titled 'Really Useless Knowledge: a political critique of Aesthetics' presents Brecht's materialist theory of art as the sole exception to centuries of idealist aesthetics, marxist or otherwise. And Terry Eagleton in his book *The Function of Criticism* offers the example of Brechtian acting style and Brecht's shrewd naivety as a model for a genuinely radical theory which must always, appropriately enough, ask the child's question 'why?' of what is apparently natural, obvious and taken for granted in the world.[1]

Brecht is invoked as a way of replying to the war-mongering appropriation of Shakespeare, as an answer to the overwhelming idealism of dominant aesthetic traditions, and as an alternative to the present lack of a public function for criticism. All three critics are witnesses to the crisis in English. Two of them, it might be said, have helped orchestrate that crisis and led the call for a politically radical, interventionist criticism to replace the only less explicitly political, liberal to conservative criticism of previous decades. Obviously Brecht is thought to have a place in making, or maintaining, an oppositional critical culture, and in general this is the recommendation I too want to make. At the same time I want to postpone further reference to Brecht so as to suggest that the approach or mentality and theory of which he is an example are not exclusively his. An alternative critical culture has in fact been in the making, as the work of Holderness, Bennett, Eagleton and others suggests. It has been building a vocabulary and syntax which, happily, find echoes, confirmation, and direction in Brecht, but which have emerged out of a very contemporary crisis. Brecht seems right now; less a *deus ex machina* than a *peripeteia*, a recovered moment in a tradition in the process of self-consciously discovering itself.

There are, however, other points of entry into this tradition and to the thinking of which Brecht is an example. Developments in English and cultural studies present one such route and I want to indicate this first. Usually, the crisis in English in its recent phase is thought to comprise a break with the moralistic defence of a minority literature and culture represented by the Leavises and *Scrutiny*. The best sketch still, I believe, of Leavis's position appeared in Perry Anderson's 'Components of the National Culture'.[2] Anderson explains there how in the absence of a tradition of British sociology or of classical marxism, which might have offered a totalizing view of society, Leavis came, with his own totalizing perspective based in selective literary values, to occupy a central place in English intellectual life. The chief merit of Anderson's account is that it helps place Leavis in a national intellectual context. He can then be seen, as Terry Eagleton suggests, as a dissident but organic intellectual, speaking from a petty bourgeois base, as Matthew Arnold had spoken at an earlier moment of crisis from a middle-class base, and from that position berating cosmopolitan literary culture and industrial society in the interests of a reformulated version of Arnold's 'better self'.[3] It was precisely because Leavis claimed that literary quality was a measure and guarantee of civilization ('a real literary interest' as he put it, 'is an interest in man, society and civilisation, and its boundaries cannot be drawn; the adjective is not a circumscribing one') that he and a version of English Studies came to occupy the cultural centre.[4] Any significant subsequent change in English therefore has been, and has to be, more than technical; more than a matter of adopting a structuralist or post-structuralist, or marxist, or feminist reading of the same traditional text. New kinds of criticism need to find a quite different institutional and cultural base from Leavis, *Scrutiny*, and Cambridge. Already it is clear that their political and intellectual inspiration derives from alternative sources: in critical theory, in forms of socialist-feminism, and in alliances, problematic though these often are, with the labour, or peace, or ecology movements; with women, blacks, or the working class.

The word crisis has been attached particularly to English, but Perry Anderson's analysis, and the necessary breath to any real change ought to make it clear that other 'components' of the culture will be drawn this way and that as the map is redrawn. 1986 is not 1968. Mrs Thatcher's England has produced right-wing intellectual pressure groups and a reactionary skin-flint ideology of education, but also alongside and contesting these, oppositional intellectual and cultural forms of a heterogeneous kind. These emergent, and of course often marginalized forms, in writing, music, publishing, theatre and in community politics have no single academic discipline

IS THERE ENGLISH AFTER CULTURAL STUDIES? 23

at their centre, and no single political party either, but exert a political influence and have points of real contact all the same, both inside and outside the educational establishment.

Amongst other things, this description applies to the forms of cultural studies which have emerged since the events of 1968 and the cultural moment of Perry Anderson's essay. Cultural studies was in so many words the invention of 1968. Its reappraisal of the concept of culture, its cross-disciplinary bias, its openness to theory, to the work of Althusser, Gramsci and Foucault, and thus to questions of ideology, discourse, and power, its later commitment to a radicalizing agenda turned consciously to questions of race, sex and class—all these, coming like successive waves of burning knowledge, have struck and endangered Fortress English, made their way inside, and assisted, from within, in the removal of Leavisite and post-Leavisite versions of English from the centre of intellectual culture.

The crisis in English can be rewritten then I think as a narrative of the changing relationship between literary and cultural criticism. In 1948, twenty years before Anderson's essay, it was possible to assume as if it were 'embarrassingly obvious'

> that the evidence which literature may provide—and it is indeed evidence that is not available elsewhere—is accessible only if the literature is treated as literature. The most scrupulous and unprejudiced response has to be made to the fact of the text; and the literature which has to be taken into account ought to be selected on its merits as literature, and not on its external relevance to the more obvious movements of history.[5]

This is not F.R. Leavis, but Raymond Williams in a forgotten book called *Reading and Criticism*. In 1969, Richard Hoggart, the first Director of the Centre for Contemporary Cultural Studies at Birmingham, revealingly titled an occasional paper *Contemporary Cultural Studies: An Approach to the Study of Literature and Society*. Hoggart's concern in this essay is entirely with how students of literature can move out from the literary text, and with the assistance of other disciplines, notably history and sociology, confirm their findings and so catch at the tone or temper of society. He speaks several times of the primacy of the literary text 'in and for itself', and often assumes the superior value of 'good' literature over popular literature and culture in a thoroughly traditional way. At the same time, however, he calls the authority of textual criticism into question in the very act of seeking alliances with other disciplines which are thought to have an explanatory reach beyond literary criticism, and at one point falls into blatant contradiction on the question of value. Thus he writes that

> it is better not to start with *a priori* divisions between types of art (high, middle, low or any of the others). It is better to start as if from scratch each time.

only then to assert that

> Lowbrow art or mass art won't yield its cultural meanings without effort. If we make that effort, we find that it can be more revealing than we would have thought; not as revealing as high art (here is where valid distinctions really do come into play— about integrity, complexity, perceptiveness) but certainly not easily read or dismissed.[6]

Subsequent work in cultural studies in the 1970s, in structuralism and marxism, in theories of ideology, in media studies, and youth cultures, served only to open these wounding contradictions further. Where once literature was thought to offer a qualitative standard, and literary criticism a model for the study of culture, their claims were shown as increasingly threadbare. English was overtaken, by foreign makes and the occasional agit-prop bus, like a steaming Morris Minor on a motorway. A resurgent marxism and varieties of post-structuralism came to inhabit the absences in British intellectual culture noted by Anderson, in the same period that the women's movement, sited both inside and outside the educational system, came to replace the student radicalism he had looked to as a major agency of social change. The theory and debates these developments engendered helped redirect the work of major socialist critics such as Raymond Williams and Terry Eagleton, and brought others to reread, subvert, or abandon the literary canon, or flee Departments of English altogether, for Departments of Film, Media, Communication, and of course Cultural Studies.

Inevitably, this process has been accompanied by an ideological critique. Traditionally, literary criticism has segmented forms of writing into what is and is not 'Literature'. Its discriminations and judgements in this field have produced an institutionalized and always selective tradition which it offers again and again as a series of reflections on the resilience and integrity of the unique individual, as evidence of both individual talent and the permanent truths of the human condition, and thus as a source of enrichment in 'our' personal lives. These are the sentiments of liberal humanism and it is no accident that Richard Hoggart titled his series of 1971 Reith lectures *Only Connect*, with its echoes of E.M. Forster writing at an earlier point of liberal crisis. When it is seen, however, that the liberal concept of the autonomous individual and the liberal doctrine of the freedom of choice can be brought to serve as conscience and apologist for the antics of a Conservative Education Minister, or for the machinations of a Rupert Murdoch in the world of 'free' enterprise, then they appear compromised and ineffective.

The attempts of literary criticism to remedy this situation only undermine its descipline boundaries. Thus, when English has looked for renewed strength and relevance in alliances with language study, history, sociology, and philosophy, it has discovered that it is itself a product of language, history, and ideology. When it has thought to extend itself to a study, for example, of Keith Joseph's speeches and writings, or to a semiology of *The Sun* newspaper, then its original methods and objects of study, its criteria of value, lose authority. If literary criticism is to be extended in this way, why not study Marvel comics and the Cold War as well as, or instead of, Milton and epic form, why not Rambo as well as Rimbaud? And why not changes in the ideology of education of which Keith Joseph was an instrument and product, or the conditions of production and reception of the capitalist press of which *The Sun* is an example? This process of self-extension, real and potential, has comprised a series of self-critiques which have unstitched the intellectual, institutional, and ideological identity of the subject. The three cherished autonomies of the text, the discipline, and the free individual have tumbled and cracked like so many Humpty Dumpties.

Terry Eagleton, as the major English literary critic after Leavis and Williams, would think this is all to the good. He argues that 'Departments of Literature in Higher Education . . . are part of the ideological apparatus of the modern capitalist state', that not only is the concept 'literature' an illusion, but that literary theory too is 'no more than a branch of social ideologies, utterly without any unity or identity'.[7] He calls, most recently, for the reappropriation of the eighteenth-century concept of literature as all writing, and of rhetoric as the study of the purposeful use of language in a return to 'the most venerable topics of criticism, before it was narrowed and impoverished to the so-called literary canon'. Instead of English and bourgeois humanist criticism we require not English, and marxist *literary* criticism, so much as 'marxist criticism' or 'political criticism'; the study of culture and signifying practices, 'a concern with the symbolic processes of social life, and the social production of forms of subjectivity'.[8] Eagleton's words find a close echo in the description of cultural studies by Richard Johnson, the present Director of the Birmingham Centre. Johnson writes that cultural studies examines the 'subjective side of social relations', the structured historical character of social forms which 'we inhabit subjectively: language, signs, ideologies, discourses, myths'.[9] The illusions of English, literature, and literary theory appear to have reached vanishing point. Instead, we have rhetoric, or in modern dress, a materialist study of signifying practices, or indeed, cultural studies.

Neither Eagleton, nor others who have argued similarly, would be naive enough to think that this is a *fait accompli*. Social ideologies persist more strenuously in real life than they do on paper, and in that real world the answer to my question 'is there English after cultural studies?' is an untidy yes and no. Conventional English obviously survives, as publishers lists, prospectuses, and personal experience tell us it does. Yet often, even while 'English' is employed as the public description of many University and Polytechnic departments, it stands above their doors, with all its ideological freight, as the false title to courses in literary and cultural theory, literature and society, American and European literature, popular literature and women's writing. This is reform rather than revolution, but the text 'in and for itself', the parochial English tradition, and the selective canon, long ago routed in theory, have in practice at least been put on the defensive. One random sign of more thoroughgoing changes appeared in an advertisement for a post in Griffith University, Brisbane, at the end of 1985. It was headed 'Text Analysis', and called for someone ('She/he') to join an interdisciplinary team, who would be 'familiar with contemporary debates in genre studies and realism theory and be able to discuss narrative conventions and character construction processes across a range of media, including literature, film and television'.

This is a job description with which many people in misnamed Departments of English or of Literature, myself included, will be quite familiar. We would do better to describe such courses as discourse analysis, or text analysis, or again, cultural studies. Often still, however, as again in my own experience, work of this kind can be introduced as a 'supplement', an in-house challenge, to more or less conventional English. If we require more of a red wedge than a soft option from this supplement, then it is not so much a matter of the name, cultural studies, as of cultural *politics*, or rather the *politics* of cultural studies.

From its elected position on the margins of the academic establishment, cultural studies offers neither a discipline, nor multi-discipline base for a reconstructed English, nor a new set of courses and texts. Instead, it presents a radicalizing mentality, both intellectual and political, which is applicable to all texts. Richard Johnson identifies this in his description of the main features of cultural studies. As a tradition this has been marked, he says, by

> its openness and theoretical versatility, its reflexive even self-conscious mood, and, especially, the importance of critique. I mean critique [Johnson stresses] in the fullest sense: not criticism merely, nor even polemic, but procedures by which other traditions are approached both for what they may yield and for what they inhibit. Critique involves stealing away the more useful elements and rejecting the rest. It involves appropriation not just rejection. From this point of view cultural studies is a process, a kind of alchemy for producing useful knowledge.[10]

Cultural studies has in this manner appropriated English (along with other disciplines and traditions), but a transformed literary studies can in turn avail itself of the method of critique, in appropriating its own past, and in the analysis of texts. Already, in both respects, literary studies has been jolted into its politicized mode. The politics of critique, in this formulation, comes with a crucial proviso, however. 'Cultural studies,' he writes, 'is not a research programme for a particular party or tendency.' Its connection with such parties or spheres of action is 'loose' and 'variable', but nonetheless 'a real one'; characterized as in the appropriation of different intellectual traditions by a 'constructive quarrel' with existing styles of political discourse and forms of action.[11]

By yet another name, critique, in its 'fullest sense', is the practice of dialectics. As described by Marx, dialectics

> is a scandal and abomination to bourgeoisdom and its doctrinaire professors because it includes in its comprehension an affirmative recognition of the existing state of things, at the same time also, the recognition of the negation of that state, of its inevitable

breaking up; because it regards every historically developed social form as in fluid movement, and therefore takes into account its transient nature not less than its momentary existence.[12]

What in particular gives this criticism its political cutting edge is the criterion enlisted by Johnson of 'really useful knowledge'. This effectively socializes the practice of evaluation, so dear to 'English' in its personal and universalizing dimensions. It disposes immediately of the sham of disinterestedness, and offers a real challenge at last to Leavis's evident 'users' for literature. The texts and values of a literary studies, so reconstituted, will be decided against the assumptions which have constructed a more or less exclusive set of largely bourgeois, white, male texts as *the* texts of Literature. As a materialist and dialectical criticism it will seek to produce a knowledge of those texts from the perspective of a continuing history, in which present needs and therefore 'useful knowledge' are defined. In the interests of which social groups, classes, and movements, we can therefore ask, however 'loose' and 'variable' the connection might be, is it worth distinguishing (to take fairly modest examples), between a traditional and feminist reading of *Jane Eyre*, between this twentieth-century utopian science fiction and that nineteenth-century realist novel, between Malcolm Bradbury and *Boys from the Blackstuff* and *Brookside*? These are questions for reconstructed literary critics, teachers and students. But others, working similarly as 'specific' intellectuals, in different areas and institutions, are also answerable to the criterion of 'useful knowledge'. Marx spoke of philosophers as only interpreting the world when the point is to change it. But this is a thesis we need now to revise as we recall it. For interpretations, or what we might prefer to call ideological constructions or representations, do have power in the world. They help define and control our place in it. A critique of dominant 'interpretations' can therefore *help* redefine and so change the world. *If* this critique and the new meanings it puts into circulation are useful, and gain consent. This is a limited, oblique, and uncertain power for change, but if modern 'philosophers', including writers, teachers, critics, and students of literary discourse, do not exercise it, they will assist in maintaining the world as it is.

Brecht attempted to adapt Marx's words to the theatre, and so, in effect, had already revised them. In answer to the question 'why Brecht?', we can now say that Brecht is 'useful' precisely because he offers a precedent for a dialectical criticism, in his theoretical essays, and quite crucially, in the domain of active cultural production. This 'critical attitude' Brecht presents in the poem 'On Judging':

> You should show what is; but also
> In showing what is you should suggest what could be and is not
> And might be successful.[13]

Its province is, interchangeably, the areas of work, cultivation, education, art and social change.

> Canalising a river
> Grafting a fruit tree
> Educating a person
> Transforming a state
> These are instances of fruitful criticism
> And at the same time
> Instances of art.[14]

Brecht's own art was an interventionist, and in his terms 'realist' art, whose object was to lay bare the real causal network of society so that it could be known and managed according to needs. Its 'realism', that is to say, consisted in its supplying 'really useful knowledge'.[15]

More specifically, his drama and poetry were founded on the device of *Verfremdung*, or 'making strange', usually misleadingly translated as 'alienation device'. This technique Brecht employed in the use of language, verse forms, song, acting style and dramaturgy in such a way that the familiar, or orthodox, the accepted and 'commonsensical' are at once shown and estranged, and thus called into question. Brecht described this process as one in which 'what is obvious is in a certain sense made incomprehensible, but this is only in order that it may be made all the easier to comprehend' (pp. 143–4). *Verfremdung* therefore describes a dialectical, critical, and artistic set of procedures, designed to surprise Brecht's readers and audience out of a passive acceptance of the way things are into an active and useful knowledge of how things might be different, or ought to change. Brecht's art was a political art therefore, but not a propagandist or agit-prop art, any more than the intellectual work I've described is the servant of a political party or group. Brecht described his theatre as 'At most, pedagogics' (p. 67); and it is to Brecht's 'usefulness' as a model for pedagogy that I want in these final remarks to particularly draw attention. The 'lessons' of his plays, as Brecht repeated, could only be completed outside the theatre. *Verfremdung*, he said, could not 'solve' the riddle of the world, only 'show' it; its object being 'to allow the spectator to criticize constructively from a social point of view' (p. 125). References to the 'critical attitude', to constructive doubt and naivety, to pedagogics, and the reversal of roles between teacher and taught, leaders and led, run like a motif through all of Brecht's writings. This thinking governed his situation as a socialist artist and intellectual, his relation to the German working-class and Communist Party, and, perhaps in the end most significantly, shaped his artistic collaboration with fellow directors, actors, designers, musicians, technicians and stage-hands. In Weimar Berlin, and in the post-war Berliner Ensemble, Brecht's chosen method of work was a collective one: 'the act of creation', he wrote in 1948, 'has now become a collective creative process, a continuum of a dialectical sort, in which the original invention taken on its own has lost much of its importance' (p. 211). Appropriately then, Brecht's late essays, titled 'Dialectics in the Theatre', are comprised of dialogues, reported discussions, and notes by other members of the Berliner Ensemble, rather than of authored essays by Brecht himself. According to one visitor the Berliner Ensemble was 'an arena of collaboration', and in another description, it 'came close to the very ideal of an artistic democracy'.[16]

This principle of collective work has of course its own pedigree, in the organizations of the working-class, the anti-authoritarian structures of the women's movement, and, not least, in the collective, provisional style of research and presentation adopted by the Birmingham Centre. There are recent signs of fragmentation and of separated projects in each of these areas; yet the principle of collective work and endeavour is a vital inheritance. A dialectical criticism and pedagogy have little hope outside of democratic structures; nor can questions of 'really useful knowledge' be put and debated without them. We have some real need then of the models and memory a supporting tradition provides, 'in a continuum of a dialectical sort'.

Notes

[1] Graham Holderness, 'Agincourt 1944: Readings in the Shakespeare Myth', *Literature and History*, 10: 1 (Spring, 1984), especially pp. 31–8; Tony Bennett, 'Really Useless "Knowledge": A Political Critique of Aesthetics',

Thesis Eleven, 12 (1985), pp. 28–52; Terry Eagleton, *The Function of Criticism* (London, 1984), pp. 89, 112. Cf. also Eagleton's *Against The Grain, Essays 1975–1985* (London, 1986), pp. 167–72.

[2] Perry Anderson, 'Components of the National Culture', *New Left Review*, 50 (1968); reprinted in *Student Power*, eds R. Blackburn and A. Cockburn (London, 1969), pp. 214–84.

[3] Cf. Terry Eagleton, *Criticism and Ideology* (London, 1976), pp. 11–21.

[4] F.R. Leavis, *The Common Pursuit* (London, 1962), p. 200.

[5] Raymond Williams, *Reading and Criticism* (London, 1950), p. 101.

[6] Richard Hoggart, *Contemporary Cultural Studies. An Approach to the Study of Literature And Society* (Birmingham, 1969), p. 13.

[7] Terry Eagleton, *Literary Theory, An Introduction* (London, 1983), pp. 200, 204.

[8] Eagleton, *The Function of Criticism*, p. 124.

[9] Richard Johnson, *What is Cultural Studies Anyway?* (Birmingham, 1983), pp. 11, 13.

[10] Johnson, pp. 1–2.

[11] Johnson, p. 8.

[12] Karl Marx, *Capital*, Vol. 1, 'Afterword to the Second German Edition' (London, 1954), p. 29.

[13] Bertolt Brecht, *Poems, 1913–1956* (London, 1976, 1981), p. 308.

[14] *Poems*, p. 309.

[15] Cf. the essay 'The Popular and the Realistic' in *Brecht on Theatre*, ed. John Willett (London, 1964), pp. 107–12. Following page references are to this volume.

[16] Quoted in Keith Dickson, *Bertolt Brecht. Towards Utopia* (London, 1978), p. 57.

Travesties of Dickens

PAUL HOGGART

The Pickwick Papers was the first real succes of Dickens's career, turning him into a celebrity and starting a kind of Pickwick 'cult'. In an age of weak copyright law, the book was openly plagiarized, imitated and plundered for names, characters and situations. *The Penny Pickwick* and *Pickwick in America* by 'Bos', and *Pickwick Abroad* by G.W.M. Reynolds, were probably the most notable and best-selling examples, but there were many other Pickwick derivatives, ranging from short novels to 'songsters' and other ephemera. *The Sketch-Book by 'Bos'*, and then *Nickelas Nickelberry*, two books called *Oliver Twiss*, one by 'Bos' and one by 'Poz', several variations on *Martin Chuzzlewhit*, and *Dombey and Daughter*, all followed.

Although some of the Pickwick imitations include paraphrasing of Dickens's writing, even occasionally direct plagiarism, most of the writing uses Dickens's characters either in parallel stories or in 'continuations' of his plot. They are best described as travesties, for they fit both modern meanings of that word. In as far as they ever attempt to emulate Dickens's style they are miserable failures; however, their real energy, and their appeal to poorer readerships than Dickens's, stems from an underlying disrespect for the emotional and ideological tenor of the original novel. In another sense they *deliberately* travesty the spirit of *The Pickwick Papers*.

The 'Bos' series was published by Edward Lloyd, the founder of a succession of mass-circulation newspapers, and although the author (probably Thomas Peckett Prest) remains obscure, their commercial success was instrumental in building up Lloyd's fiction business, which in turn provided the capital for his newspaper empire. *Pickwick Abroad* was G.W.M. Reynolds's first successful book (it was extensively and favourably reviewed in middle-brow journals). Reynolds became, briefly, prominent in the Chartist movement, but is now remembered as the author of two enormous serial novels, *The Mysteries of London* and *The Mysteries of the Court of London*, both of which were best-sellers, and as the founder of *Reynolds' Weekly*, which survived until the 1960s.

Mr Pickwick, then, launched three exceptionally successful

careers, not one, and in some respects the imitations are milestones in the history of commercial popular fiction. Since this is a history which receives very little academic attention (though there are some important exceptions, such as the work of Louis James), they have tended merely to be noted as quirky Dickensiana, feeble attempts by talentless hacks to jump on Dickens's bandwagon. There is *some* validity in this view, but it provides no explanation of their popularity. This popularity needs to be explained because the books were written at a time of cultural transition, in which authors and publishers were developing styles, conventions and ideological formulae which were to dominate commercial literature for years to come.

The different versions of Pickwick, in fact, provide a fascinating case study in the relationships between popular writing and the 'serious' writing that constitutes 'literature' courses. *The Pickwick Papers* is of course generally regarded as a light novel, but it is also taken up by many critics insofar as it opens out many of the moral and social preoccupations of Dickens's later works. Popular literature, on the other hand, remains largely unexplored, despite recent shifts in the theoretical orientation of many critics, which might reasonably have been expected to open this area up. At this stage it is perhaps worth considering why this should be the case, since any attempt to compare commercial literature with more serious writing is bound to raise basic questions about the nature and purpose of literary analysis.

Throughout the 1960s and 70s literary critics remained, on the whole, indifferent or actively hostile to the ferment of philosophical perspectives influencing related disciplines such as cultural or media studies. There were, of course, structuralist, post-structuralist and Lacanian critics, but their work tended to be marginalized. Recently a more coherent body of such criticism has begun to develop under the umbrella of 'cultural materialism',[1] but even the new criticism remains overwhelmingly preoccupied with the canon of texts already on university courses. This betrays, I believe, certain problems inherent in the relationship between the more radical approaches and traditional criticism, which remain unresolved.

Established forms of criticism tend to be based on one or more of the following tenets. First, great literature has a unique capacity to recreate imaginatively the quality of human experience. It can therefore increase our understanding of the lives of individuals and societies far beyond the range of direct personal experience.

Second, literature can provide direct *commentary* on the life of societies, seen with a fullness unavailable in other disciplines which are circumscribed by artificial divisions between categories of experience. In a great novel questions of history, psychology, sociology, and philosophy are fused in an organic whole. Literature is then to be valued according to the insight and seriousness with which this is achieved.

Third, great literature reveals to us what is universal in human nature and thus immeasurably deepens our collective self-knowledge. This universality, it is argued, explains the popularity of certain great writers in the most diverse cultures.

Finally, the aesthetic appreciation of literature is seen as an end in itself. It is the critic's role to cultivate the ability to understand and savour even finer works. For many critics, a writer's level of intellectual sophistication is an integral part of her or his work's capacity to afford pleasure. Writing which is clumsy or superficial has no real interest.

Every one of these premises is directly challenged by one or more of the 'cultural materialist' approaches. The central categories of 'experience' and 'universality', for instance, are identified as naive and misleading illusions, masking the processes by which reality is constructed. Far from accepting the artist as commentator, Althusserian and Gramscian Marxists stress the specific role of all cultural production within broader social and ideological conflicts. Various forms of structuralism stress, not the individuality of texts, but their dependence on the linguistic and cultural systems within which they are formed. The question of an author's intention, central to traditional criticism, is regarded with scepticism or as a complete irrelevance within these perspectives. The history and practice of literary criticism has become itself the object of analysis. Accepting the premises of these theoretical approaches enforces a certain analytical stringency. It becomes simply inadequate to discuss a Shakespeare play, for example, without taking into account the material conditions of its production. An analysis of Joyce's writing *must* address its deliberate rupture of linguistic discourse.

The difficulty is that, while transforming our understanding of great texts, these approaches tend to undermine the very reasons for studying them in the first place. Jonathan Dollimore touches on this dilemma in his introduction to *Political Shakespeare*:

One of the most important achievements of 'theory' in English studies has been the making possible of a truly interdisciplinary approach to—some might say exit from—the subject. (p.2)

As elements in systems of signification, or as components in complex ideological superstructures, literary works lose their privileged status as unique recreations of experience. They become interesting and significant, not as diagnoses of consciousness, but as symptoms of it.

This implication has tended to reinforce the suspicion and hostility of orthodox critics to the new perspectives. It has presented the cultural materialist critic with a more uncomfortable choice, for logically it should lead to a re-examination of the entire basis of literary study, in which the centrality of the canon has to be established on a new basis, or abandoned. Some critics have indeed 'exited from the subject' into areas of cultural studies or sociology. More, however, have sought to maintain the value of literary study by discovering in particular texts disruptive or subversive interventions in the discourses of their period.

On the whole, however, there is a tendency to skirt around this problem altogether. Both Terry Eagleton and Raymond Williams have done this at various times. In his 'Afterword' to *Political Shakespeare*, Williams argues that we should continue to study the 'mainstream' because of these works' 'substantial importance' (which is not defined) and because of 'their formation into what has been called a canon' (p. 236).

None of these responses seems really satisfactory. While many texts may be, in some respects, disruptive or subversive, many more are not, and if this kind of ideological struggle is of the essence, why confine the analysis to texts which have already become established on literature courses because they fulfilled wholly different criteria? Isn't it too much of a coincidence that broadly the same texts should be of 'substantial importance' to someone looking to Brecht, Barthes, Althusser, Gramsci, Foucault or Lacan as to a follower of Empson or Leavis? While I agree with Williams's argument that the formation of canons is significant in itself, this can hardly be seen as a substitute for the study of the *inherent* importance of works of literature at the heart of a three-year degree course.

It seems to me that *all* literary production is part of a broader conflict, both across societies and through time, around the meanings of 'signs' and how such signs are ideologically charged. No writing can take place in isolation and every adaptation of a convention, reworking of a character type, variation of linguistic style, is, in itself, an intervention in this process.

By 'signs' I mean, loosely, the 'para-language' defined by Barthes,[2] the raw materials of cultural exchange which can encompass anything from a hand-gesture, to a type of joke, from a conventional character-type in a work of fiction to an entire literary genre.

There are many different *types* of conflict around signs, but it is possible to distinguish between two main kinds: those arising from genuine hostility between ideologies that are, at root, incompatible, and those which, while *appearing* to be hostile, are in fact complementary. (The anti-intellectualism of *The Sun*, for instance, appears to demonstrate hostility to middle-class values, but forms an element in a kind of right-wing populism that dovetails excellently with right-wing middle-class attitudes.)

It therefore seems a shame that literary critics are not more willing to broaden their field of vision to encompass popular literature, and indeed other popular cultural forms, since this could only deepen our understanding of the role any particular text was playing in the broader cultural debate. The point about the various reworkings of *The Pickwick Papers* is that, because the authors raided Dickens's raw materials, the struggles over the meanings of signs (it doesn't really matter whether these are conscious or not) take place in the open, on the surface of the texts.

The introduction to the bound volume of *The Penny Pickwick* in the British Library claims sales of 50,000 per week. If this is accurate, the book was out-selling Dickens. Even it it is only partially accurate, it is likely that the book had far more working-class readers than *The Pickwick Papers*, which had a predominantly middle-class readership. The author is quite open in his targeting of a working-class audience. 'The poor too', he writes, 'should have their Momus.' This was only possible because working-class literacy rates were remarkably high. One study of a poor inner London area at about this time found over 50% of the adult population competent in basic reading and writing. Newspapers and serial fiction were often read aloud communally, at work and in coffee-houses or gin-shops, so that audiences were always likely to exceed actual sales.

Studies like Richard Altick's *The English Common Reader*, have documented the wide, if erratic, range of education then available to the working-classes.[3] This was broadly divided into two types: a motley array of self-help schools, with rudimentary Dame Schools at one extreme and much more organized Sunday schools at the other, and the schooling provided by concerned but missionizing middle-class organizations.

This duality was reflected in the literature available to the poor in the early years of the century. There had been, for example, a thriving radical press which went 'underground' in defiance of the loosely enforced Stamp Act and continued to appear illegally unstamped until 1836 when the Whig government began to enforce a reduced Stamp Duty much more vigorously. On the other hand, lower class readers were beset by endless supplies of 'improving tracts' from the numerous individuals and institutions concerned with their moral and spiritual welfare.

What was not particularly evident before 1836 was massproduced literature written primarily to *entertain*. This changed rapidly as the government moved against the unstamped press, since proprietors were forced to fill their periodicals with invented police reports and other forms of light entertainment to replace now illegal news. Gradually the size of the potential market for such material became clear to publishers, who produced ever-increasing quantities of criminal adventures, gothic melodramas and various forms of humour. The origins of these new forms of mass-market literature lay, not so much in the literature and periodicals that they were supplanting, as in the chap-books, ballads and broadsheets of the eighteenth century. The Pickwick imitations were among the most successful publications to be produced as this development occurred, so their ideological make-up has a particular historical significance.

Middle-class publishing too was in a period of transition and the story of how *The Pickwick Papers* came into being illustrates this well. Chapman and Hall were aware of the growing market for serial publication of a light kind and were searching for an illustrator and writer to produce a series of comic 'sporting' scenes. The list of artists and writers who were considered for text and drawings seems endless and included both Thackeray and, for the pictures, Alfred Crowquill who was to illustrate (badly) Reynolds's *Pickwick Abroad*. The idea was really derived from the comical style of Surtees's Jorrocks stories in which early nineteenth-century lower-middle-class man attempts to emulate the life of an eighteenth-century country squire. The original conception of the Pickwick club therefore lay in the encounter between the ever more numerous and self-confident middle-class suburbanite and the culture of the rural gentry. The informing joke revolved around suburban man's inept search for a sense of identity.

Dickens was only offered the work after several more established writers had turned it down and even then he was merely to provide a text to the sketches which were the focus of the exercise. Dickens's only previous literary work, as opposed to pure journalism, had been *Sketches by Boz*, which had explored the by-ways of urban and suburban life in a manner quite unlike Surtees. In fact, the artist, Seymour, struggled with the work and grew suicidally depressed as Dickens's text began to capture the attention of readers.

Dickens was extremely skilled at imitation and pastiche, and the sudden and intense popularity of his writing was largely due to the skill with which the minutiae of early-Victorian culture were reproduced and ridiculed. Much of this humour is completely lost on the modern reader who must wade through dense footnotes to discover, for instance, that Mr Blotton's speech in chapter one is a direct parody of a contemporary parliamentary row, but this quality in the book is repeatedly referred to by contemporary reviewers.

Henry James wrote of Dickens's 'command of the permeable air and the collective sensibility'. We may wish to limit this by defining *whose* collective sensibility (the world of Mayhew's London appears in Dickens only as a threatening 'other' and he seems to have loathed the upper classes), but his Victorian readers undoubtedly relished his tight and detailed recreation of their culture, which included not only a parade of recognizable and probably hackneyed 'types' (tricksters, would-be poets, medical students, choleric army officers), but also, through the inset tales and many incidents in the main narrative, a kaleidoscope of popular cultural forms. This quality itself overlaid a structure of narrative largely derived from eighteenth-century fiction. '*The Pickwick Papers*, in fact, are made up of two pounds of Smollet, three ounces of Sterne, a handful of Hook, a dash of a grammatical Pierce Egan', wrote a reviewer in *The Athenaeum*. There is a minor industry devoted to tracing the sources of Dickens's art and *Pickwick* is one of the deepest mines.

This may explain the book's short-term popularity, but not its grip up to Dickens's death and beyond. (The author of *The Times* obituary insisted that it was his best book.) The long-term popularity of the book was far more profound and was due, not to the fact that Dickens had a sharp eye for cultural signs and enjoyed playing around with them, but to the manner in which he transformed them. Sales of the instalments did not really take off until the introduction of Sam Weller. Sam, needless to say, introduced a kind of salty working-class humour (though it is worth noting that it is both gentle and genteel compared to some of the humour then being produced for working-class readers), but it was the introduction of the master/servant relationship that allowed the disparate elements of the story to cohere.

There are two central 'signifiers' in *The Pickwick Papers*. Both had their own history and both were given a new and potent ideological significance as the narrative developed. The first signifier is the figure of Mr Pickwick himself and the second is the master/servant relationship between Mr Pickwick and Sam.

The figure of the tubby, pompous, somewhat irascible elderly man was entirely familiar to Dickens's readers. He was familiar from literature and also felt to correspond to real human beings. A reviewer in the *Metropolitan Magazine* identified him thus, 'encased in a good coating of aldermanic fur, and instead of spear and sword, has his own powers of declamation with which to go forth and do fearful battle . . .' It was Dickens's original intention to imitate the style of Surtees in which the purpose of this character's existence is primarily to be the butt of callous slapstick humour. In the early chapters Mr Pickwick is subjected to a series of physical humiliations, culminating in his spell in the dog-pound. His reactions are brittle, short-tempered and self-important. Like his predecessors, he is, at this stage, an unlikeable figure. Like the other members of the Pickwick Club his pretensions are ludicrous. His dissertation on the source of the Hampstead Ponds is as absurd a suburbanite's fantasy as Winkle's claims to sportsmanship. The opening reference to him as 'the immortal Pickwick', which comes to acquire an air of truth as the narrative closes, is at this stage entirely ironical.

After the arrival of Sam, Mr Pickwick's ignorance and gullibility become gradually transmuted into innocence and guilelessness:

> 'Can such things be!' exclaimed the astonished Mr Pickwick.
> 'Lord bless your heart, sir,' said Sam, 'why where was you half baptized?—that's nothin' that a'nt.' (ch. 13)

Gradually generosity and an indiscriminate benevolence replace the original truculence and the pomposity becomes a kind of dogged moral strength. This reaches a peak during the trial episode, through Mr Pickwick's defiance of the crooked lawyers and his decision to go to prison rather than pay the damages unjustly awarded against him.

Exposed to human misery in the debtors' prison, Mr Pickwick develops new dimensions of social compassion.

Orwell, in his famous essay[4], notes the absence of descriptions of *work* in Dickens's novels. Dickens, he claims, did not really know very much about how people earned their money. Only the vaguest hints are dropped as to the origin of Mr Pickwick's wealth. He is supposed to have been in some form of business, but this sits uncomfortably with his extreme innocence of the world. The whole tenor of the narrative suggests that Mr Pickwick's money is a sort of gift of Providence. Mr Pickwick is well-off because he deserves to be—because he is good.

Mr Pickwick began life as a sign of suburban man seen as a rather absurd and clueless figure, ineptly posing as something more glorious and interesting than he could ever be. By the end of the book he has *become* glorious. Dickens has provided the identity that was missing; the shortcomings have been translated into radiant virtues. Dickens has provided for his middle-class, often suburban, readership a figure who transforms their own limitations into strengths and who offers a blanket validation of their own comfort and complacency. As a conscious idea this is absurd, but as a *sign* Mr Pickwick tells us that wealth and goodness go together more powerfully than any political tract.

If Mr Pickwick is a kind of apotheosis of middle-class suburban man, his relationship with Sam extends this into the realm of relations between classes. Dickens was conscious of the echo of Don Quixote and Sancho Panza, which presumably suggested the division of labour between the spirit and the flesh. Sam is 'streetwise'; he educates Mr Pickwick in the ways of the world, but never loses his deference or respect. He recognizes Mr Pickwick's moral earnestness and spiritual goodness.

Sam is in some ways associated closely with Dickens's own voice. This becomes particularly clear on such occasions as the introduction of the medical students (ch. 30). Sam introduces them to Mr Pickwick, Dickens to his readers, but Dickens and Sam employ a rhetoric, ironic and wry, which is essentially identical. Sam is, in effect, a native guide on Mr Pickwick's anthropological expedition through society. But, whereas he introduces a world of doss-houses and cheating servants to Mr Pickwick and the reader, he makes it all seem amusing and palatable. He cushions the shock.

Sam's shrewdness is paramount. Tony Weller states, 'I always thought that the names of Veller and gammon could never come into contract, Sammy, never' (ch. 23). He flatters the poorer reader with an English Figaro-character, competent and lucidly articulate, who looks on with wry detachment at the buffooneries of master and friends. Unlike Figaro, however, Sam supports his master. They bind together in a sentimental endorsement of social relationships which are essentially feudal. Mr Pickwick is proud of Sam because he is an 'original'; their complementary strengths provide an emotional justification of the social system. The whole narrative thus becomes a sign of a harmonious social order, through the two central characters' triumph over adversity.

Turning to the two major imitations of *Pickwick*, *The Penny Pickwick* and *Pickwick Abroad*, two important points quickly become apparent. Firstly, both 'Bos' and Reynolds responded to the diverse cultural satire of *The Pickwick Papers* and sought to produce versions of it which they felt would appeal to their own readerships. These were not the same: *The Penny Pickwick* was consciously aimed at working-class readers, whereas Reynolds seems to have been primarily interested in a lower-middle-class readership. Secondly, it is repeatedly apparent that the authors have recognized in Dickens's writing the existing cultural forms on which Dickens's characters and incidents are based and are providing alternative versions of those forms rather than attempting to copy Dickens's versions of them directly.

This process is perhaps most neatly illustrated in the naming of the town where the election episodes occur in Dickens and 'Bos'. Dickens's depiction of the election followed a tradition of election scenes, the most notable of which was probably Hogarth's series of paintings. He named his borough Eatanswill and the 'Bos' name, Guzzleton, appears to be a paraphrase of this, until we notice that the name on an election placard in the second painting of Hogarth's sequence is Guzzledown. Dickens transforms Hogarth's election in one way; 'Bos' goes back to it and transforms it in another.

There is a good deal of consistency in the ways in which 'Bos' and Reynolds rework the raw cultural material of *The Pickwick Papers*, although they differ somewhat from each other. The language of *The Penny Pickwick* immediately signals the difference in tone. Dickens's ornate, Latinate style was, to a certain extent, mock-heroic, but there is such evident pleasure in the very elaboration of the sentences that the style becomes a celebration as well as a parody. 'Bos' on the other hand insists on a bathetic contrast between the lengthy sentence, peppered with poly-syllabic vocabulary, and a mundane, if not grim, reality. It is worth comparing his opening passages with Dickens's famous opening. *The Penny Pickwick* begins:

> Previous to the year 1817, the science of this sublunary world was of that narrow and circumscribed description, that it might be looked upon merely as a small rushlight, glimmering in a dark lantern, shedding but a flickering beam upon the illiterate inhabitants. It rested with one man to dissipate that dulness [sic]—to expand the rushlight of intellectual research into the full blaze and overwhelming brilliancy of the gas-light of wisdom. (p. 1)

The passage proceeds in a welter of references to Charlies, Peelers, baked-potato venders and gin-palaces.

The attitude to language is paralleled by the presentation both of cultural forms and of events and characters in the narrative. 'Bos', like Dickens, provides parodies of contemporary genres, but they are fundamentally out of sympathy in a way which Dickens's parodies never really are. Again, the element of celebration which enabled Dickens, in a sense, to 'have it both ways', is missing from *The Penny Pickwick*. A good example is an incident, unrelated to anything in *The Pickwick Papers*, in which Christopher Pickwick accompanied by Samivel Veller, visits Daniel Dreary, a sort of Thomas Love Peacock figure, at Dreary Hall. The Gothic style is crudely parodied, but in such a way that it is seen merely as an incomprehensible freak of middle-class life.

Generally 'Bos' writes with an insistent crudeness. The slapstick, like that of Dickens's predecessors, is often raw and brutal: the edges are harsh. Far from softening the roughness of the low-life he describes, as Dickens does, 'Bos' revels in it. This is well illustrated in his version of the election scene when Sir Gregory Graspall, a candidate, makes his speech:

> 'Electors of Guzzleton, this is the most glorious moment of my political career! (Bah! Bah! hisses! groans and a torrent of mud). Gentlemen your kind reception overwhelms me (A knock in the eye with a rotten orange). Gentlemen, I stand here to receive—' (a dead cat thrown plump at Sir Gregory's head). (p. 131)

As each incident and as each character is paralleled, 'Bos' avoids the cosier constructions of Dickens's novel, providing a version which, although usually badly written, is liable to come closer to the spirit of the material from which Dickens derived his narrative, and in the case of the many rascals and ruffians who populate the story, which probably comes a lot closer to the reality of early Victorian low-life. There is frequently a real relish in the humiliations these characters are able to inflict on Mr Pickwick.

Christopher Pickwick remains pompous and bad-tempered. Unlike Dickens's character he never really acquires grace. Samivel Veller, on the other hand, remains more detached and aloof. He shares Sam Weller's role as the shrewd and knowing common man, but has no emotional commitment to the master/servant relationship. The relationship is accepted as a fact of life, but seen from below, as it were, it attracts a different set of myths. The values of the middle-class masters are eccentric foibles, best viewed with dry detachment. The lower classes are better off as they are, inherently superior, even though their masters will never understand this.

Dickens's ideological loading of Pickwick and his relationship to his servant is rejected by 'Bos', but the ideological loading which 'Bos' substitutes is really complementary, for it provides an alternative construction of the status quo within which working-class readers are offered a comforting sense of *their* identity, quite different from the one offered in Dickens's work.

Reynolds's presentation of the Sam–Pickwick relationship is broadly similar to that of 'Bos', as is his attitude to the Pickwickians. Their humiliations in *Pickwick Abroad* almost always arrive as punishments for various forms of moral weakness, in fact.

Where Reynolds differs from both Dickens and 'Bos' is in his attempt to supply an alternative frame of cultural reference. Reynolds had lived in France, where *Pickwick Abroad* takes place, and uses the book to introduce elements of French popular culture which he felt to be racy and sophisticated. He was beginning to define the style and preoccupations that made up his later novels. Reynolds also used the novel to inform his readers about various forms of English criminal life of which he seems to have had considerable knowledge. It is, on the whole, a voyeuristic interest aimed primarily at lower-middle-class readers who wished to feel they were 'in the know', and thus occupies a terrain somewhere between Dickens and 'Bos'.

The contrasts of style and tone between the various Pickwick texts stem from more deep-seated ideological differences. These are not straightforward. They are born of the processes by which social groups competed over a currency of cultural materials, whose meanings were reworked to establish senses of identity and social position in a rapidly changing world.

Notes

[1] See, for example, Jonathan Dollimore, *Political Shakespeare* (Manchester, 1985), pp. vii–viii.

[2] See Roland Barthes, *Mythologies* (London, 1972).

[3] Richard D. Altick, *The English Common Reader* (Chicago, 1957).

[4] George Orwell, 'Charles Dickens' in *Inside the Whale* (London, 1940).

The Mystique of the Bachelor Gentleman in Late Victorian Masculine Romance

MICHAEL SKOVMAND

The above title, in all its conceptual density, should indicate the multiple aim of the following: to suggest, by concrete analysis, how, within the theoretical horizon of a cultural studies approach, notions of gender and class may be conceived of within a specific historical period, privileging as material for study a particular kind of literature.

Obviously, the number and magnitude of the questions raised leave room for only a cursory examination: the notion of 'masculine romance', the peculiarities of the late Victorian period, complex notions of the 'gentleman' and 'gentility', and bachelorhood on top of that, all of this can only be looked into in a preliminary way.

Nevertheless, always running the risk of biting off more than is chewable in one article of this length, my intention is deliberately synoptic: to take a walk round the estate of the late Victorian bachelor gentleman—a cultural configuration that is at once literary, sociological, historiographic. In short, this is a *cultural studies* project, conceptually reuniting what was really never separate, except in the minds of overspecialized scholars.

'The Way of All Flesh': a limit case

On the face of it, it may seem odd to take as my point of departure a work like Samuel Butler's *The Way of All Flesh* (1903), the posthumous semi-autobiography which stands as the classic rejection of the entire Victorian *Weltanschauung*: duty, self-denial, celebration of the nuclear family, rigid observance of propriety, etc. Superficially, this would categorize *The Way of All Flesh* as an early modern novel about 'the man who got away',[1] alongside the early works of say James Joyce or D.H. Lawrence. However, whereas Butler's point of *departure* is the rejection of Victorian mores, his point of *arrival* nevertheless is one of the predominant ideological constructions of the late Victorian period: the haven of the bachelor gentleman. By the end of the novel, Overton, narrator and bachelor uncle of Ernest Pontifex, the protagonist, has merged not only with the authorial position of Samuel Butler, but also with the by now middle-aged Ernest Pontifex, all three of them having arrived at comfortable gentlemanly bachelorhood. Ernest's working-class wife and untidy children have been negotiated away in an acceptable fashion, and the problem of work has been taken care of through the intervention of a nice inheritance from an aunt.

As Richard Hoggart points out in his introduction to the 1966 Penguin edition, *The Way of All Flesh*, like so many other autobiographies in fictional form, is characterized by the 'selective perception' of someone whose interest is not simply description but vindication, and perhaps even revenge. There is emotion in excess of the fact, and the displacements and overreactions arising out of this are in themselves a fascinating object of study. However, more interesting in this context is the significant absence of one of the concomitants of bachelorhood, viz. the area of extramarital sex. Hoggart points out how Butler himself paid weekly visits to a woman called 'Madame' for sexual relief, combined with his sexually ambiguous male friendships. No such relief is granted to Ernest Pontifex of *The Way of All Flesh*. For one thing, the proximity between Ernest and Samuel Butler would make this kind of intimacy unacceptable. But also, I would suggest, this kind of revelation would go against the *subtext* of *The Way of All Flesh*, the 'masculine romance' of Ernest Pontifex: the story of how Sir Ernest, after languishing in the citadel of the Victorian Nuclear Family, smote the dragon Hypocrisy, and, aided by aunts and uncles, rid himself of the manacles of Wife and Children, in order to enter the blessed garden of Leisured Bachelorhood. The dispassionate 'scientific' analysis of the Victorian family in the *novel The Way of All Flesh* is at odds with the subtext of the *romance*, in which His Majesty the Ego, as Freud put it,[2] is the hero.

The consciousness of a generic distinction between novel and romance goes back to the beginnings of prose fiction, but is given a particular inflection in the late Victorian period. R.L. Stevenson, Rider Haggard, George Saintsbury and others saw themselves as part of a 'romantic revival', in polemic against the 'school' of realism/naturalism of Henry James and Zola (which was not in any sense a school, indeed James is cited as having characterized Zola's *Nana* as 'unutterably filthy'!). The writer of romance, according to Stevenson, shows us the realisation and the apotheosis of the daydreams of common men. His stories may be nourished with the realities of life, but their true mark is to satisfy the nameless longings of the reader and to obey the ideal laws of the daydream.[3]

The ambiguous position of romance within the hierarchies of literary taste is tied up with the class aspect of romance. Romance is intrinsically a mode of storytelling, an oral mode. The aura of the novelist as *auteur*, creator, privileges the novelist in relation to his audience, which are positioned not as participants, but as consumers of the narrative. The storyteller of popular/romance narrative, conversely, is, at least originally, without the aura of the creator. He is only invested with a provisional competence by having previously been in the position of listener, and in the act of telling he passes on this competence to his audience.[4]

Northrop Frye's definition of popular literature as 'what people read without guidance from their betters' is an apposite one in this context. Frye's *The Secular Scripture, A Study of the Structure of Romance* (1976) underscores this proletarian/popular aspect of romance:

> Any serious discussion of romance has to take into account its curiously proletarian status as a form generally disapproved of, in most ages, by the guardians of taste and learning, except when they use it for their own purposes.[5] (p. 23)

For Frye, when romance is so used by 'the guardians' it is appropriate to speak of 'kidnapped romance' which

> expresses that aristocracy's dreams of its own social function, and the idealized acts of protection and responsibility that it invokes to justify that function. Haggard . . . and John Buchan and Rudyard Kipling . . . incorporate the dreams of British Imperialism. This is the process of what we call 'kidnapping' romance, the absorbing of it into the ideology of an ascendant class. (p. 57)

Frye, however, is less than precise about the class aspect of late Victorian 'kidnapped' romance. Roger Bromley[6] is right in emphasizing the 'aristocratic façade' of romance, and the doubleness involved in its being *bourgeois* dreams of an aristocratic way of life, dreams which in his view serve to *legitimize* and *naturalize* distinctions of class and sex.

Any discussion whether Frye is right in seeing late Victorian masculine romance as an originally popular form kidnapped for hegemonic purposes, or whether Bromley is right in seeing popular romance as by definition part of the legitimizing process of the ruling class, is absurd once one considers the sheer range of masculine romance, from the middle-brow revivalism of Stevenson 'down' to the mass-formulaic penny dreadfuls. Masculine romance (which is Bromley's term) in the late Victorian period, should rather be seen as a mode of negotiating, in the age of British Imperialism and Darwinism, the three major upheavals of the time: The New Woman; the ascent of the working classes; and the massive urbanization of Britain, with its concomitant alienation, and visibility of vice and social misery.

In 1890, Arthur Conan Doyle, the father of the most famous bachelor gentleman of the period, wrote an essay on 'Mr Stevenson's Methods in Fiction'[7] in which he pointed to what he saw as Stevenson's only limitation, the fact that 'there is no female interest. We feel that it is an apotheosis of the boy's story—the penny number of our youth *in excelsis*'. Doyle went on to point out how 'The modern masculine novel ... marks the reaction against the abuse of love in fiction'. In many ways Doyle is right in pointing to this lack of 'female interest'. A story like *Dr Jeckyll and Mr Hyde* (1886) is essentially a story about the world of bachelor doctors and lawyers. The central focus of interest is Dr Jekyll's inability to reconcile the social image of the successful scientist with the private self of the bachelor seeking sexual relief with prostitutes. As Dr Jekyll puts it in his 'Full Statement of the Case':

> Many a man would have even blazoned such irregularities as I was guilty of; but from the high views that I had set before me, I regarded and hid them with an almost morbid sense of shame. It was thus rather the exacting nature of my aspirations, than any particular degradation in my faults, that made me what I was and, with even a deeper trench than the majority of men, severed in me those provinces of good and ill which divide and compound man's dual nature. (p. 81)

The sexual 'irregularity' of the bachelor gentleman is the subtext of *Dr Jekyll and Mr Hyde*, and although the story was used in many a Victorian sermon as a warning against the unleashing of the 'lower' desires within us all, in fact Stevenson's message is the opposite:

people should come to terms with their sexuality; if they fail to do so, the consequence may be the schizophrenia of Dr Jekyll/Mr Hyde.

Of course, neither prostitutes nor sex are referred to in any direct way. A range of euphemisms are used: 'undignified pleasures', 'shame', 'irregularities', etc. But prostitution was a major industry in late Victorian London, and no one can have had any doubt as to what those 'undignified pleasures' referred to. Also, while the sexual explorers of the Jekyll/Hyde description were looking for undignified pleasures, a wave of (upper) middle class social explorers went into the East End and similar jungles of urban misery. Their findings, and their indignation, at least modified the complacency of the Victorian political establishment through their revelations of the unacceptable face of the domestic side of Victorian Imperialism.[8]

'Gentrification'

The mystique of the bachelor gentleman in the late Victorian period is tied up with a complex of historical developments which are related to changing class relations as well as to changes in family structures and gender relations.

Perry Anderson and Tom Nairn have pointed out 'there was from the start no fundamental antagonistic contradiction between the old aristocracy and the new bourgeoisie'.[9] Instead there was accommodation, a kind of merger, in which the *rentier* aristocracy maintained a cultural hegemony the result of which was the 'gentrification'[10] of the bourgeoisie. The nineteenth century construction of 'the English way of life' is essentially rural and 'leisured', an aristocratic construction in stark contrast to the massive industrialization and urbanization of the period.

The concept of the gentleman then, as it developed through the nineteenth century, came to embody a social ideal which mediated between aristocratic and middle-class values. Indeed, it was seen as a moral code *transcending* class distinctions. Philip Mason[11] points to four distinct types emerging in the Victorian period: the officer and gentleman; the scholar and gentleman; the Christian gentleman; and the gentleman sportsman. Mason and others argue that the widening of the concept of the gentleman in the nineteenth century, away from its class connotations and into the behavioural *je ne sais quoi* which persists even today, was required in order to expand the base of recruitment for the growing number of intermediate level leaders needed in the hierarchies of industry and empire.

The emergence and expansion of the Arnoldian public school as 'the factory for gentlemen'[12] is an indication of the social and educational strategies involved in becoming a gentleman, but also an indication of the inherent class bias of the term. However at the beginning of the century the number of public schools was nine; by 1914 it had risen to nearly three hundred. The Arnoldian philosophy, with its emphasis on mental and bodily discipline, particularly through sports, and its bias against anything 'useful' such as science or engineering, not only determined the outlook of the gentlemen issuing from these institutions, but permeated the entire educational system, aided by such fictional celebrations as *Tom Brown's Schooldays* (1856).

Along with the 'gentrification' of the middle classes there was another development of major importance: the *professionalization* of a whole range of middle-class occupations. The traditional professional men—doctors, lawyers—became organised (The Law Society in 1825, the British Medical Association in 1856), and new professions emerged: civil engineers (1818), architects (1834), pharmacists (1841) etc. Between 1841 and 1881, the seventeen main professional occupations increased their numbers by 150 per cent, compared to a general rise in population of 60 per cent. However, unlike developments in the United States and on the continent, the professions were to a great extent separated from commerce and industry. As Matthew Arnold put it in a report (1868) 'in no country . . . do the professions so naturally and generally share the cast of ideas of the aristocracy as in England'.[13] The 'anticapitalist' values of the 'gentrified' professional classes were profoundly dysfunctional in relation to the needs of the expanding sectors of commerce and industry. In fact according to Wiener, 'the rooting of pseudoaristocratic attitudes and values in upper-middle class educated opinion' in the second half of the nineteenth century is the main reason why Britain lost its competitive edge against particularly Germany and the United States, and thus the root cause of Britain's present social and economic malaise.

As the century progressed the concept of gentleman grew more and more idealized. From being a powerful vehicle of social identification in the mid-Victorian society of rising expectations, it became increasingly defensive: the self-image of the beleaguered middle-class male facing the emergence of the New Woman, the organization of the working classes, and internationally the Imperialist scramble for territory in the face of growing competition on the world market. One of the indications of this development is the revival of the notion of chivalry. As Mark Girouard points out in *The Return to Camelot: Chivalry and the English Gentleman* (1981), whereas at the beginning of the century the notion of the chivalrous gentleman would have been virtually meaningless, by the end of the century a gentleman simply had to be chivalrous or he was no gentleman at all.

> A chivalrous gentleman was brave, straightforward and honourable, loyal to his monarch, country and friends, unfailingly true to his word, ready to take issue with anyone he saw ill-treating a woman, child or animal. He was a natural leader of men, and others unhesitatingly followed his lead. He was fearless in war and on the hunting-field, and excelled at all manly sports; but, however tough with the tough, he was invariably gentle to the weak; above all, he was always tender, respectful and courteous to women, regardless of their rank. (p. 260)

This sounds like a quotation from a Boy Scout manual, and indeed the formation of boys' brigades in the eighties and nineties and of course Robert Baden-Powell's immensely popular Boy Scout Movement around the turn of the century drew heavily on the concept of the chivalrous gentleman, in combination with the more woodcraft-oriented American organizations, Woodcraft Indians and the Knights of King Arthur.

Drawing on what was essentially a public schoolboy ethos, these organizations were mainly designed for the edification of working-class and lower middle-class boys. Masturbation and fornication were the two chief dragons to be slain, particularly within the Young Knights of the Alliance of Honour, founded in 1903 and concerned primarily with the preservation of sexual purity. Young Knights were told to think of 'the sacredness of your sister's body', whenever they were falling into temptation. In *Scouting for Boys* (1908) Baden-Powell gave advice on 'beastliness', cold water being suggested as a remedy.

The pseudo-medievalism of this concept of the chivalrous gentleman was only one aspect of a broad movement of conservatism, preservationism and retrenchment in this period. The revivalism within the arts (Gothic architecture, the medievalism of the Arts and Crafts movement, the preservation of practically anything 'time-honoured'), all this boiled down to

First, a loss of confidence in the creative powers of one's contemporaries and an elevation of past over present; second, a highly critical view of industrial capitalism and its 'materialistic' ethos.[14]

One may speculate as to how the proliferation of the ideal of the chivalrous gentleman affected actual lived sexuality during the period. As Steven Marcus has pointed out (*The Other Victorians*, 1974), during the late Victorian period pornography was published in unprecedented volume. Prostitution was a major social fact, massively present for everyone to see in all urban areas of any size. On the other hand, as argued by Edward Shorter[15], a major revolution had taken place, beginning in the early nineteenth century, to do with the 'sentimentalization' of courtship, marriage and child care. Former pragmatic modes of premarital and marital relations gave way to the sentiment of romantic love; communal ties were weakened with the development of the modern nuclear family, with its premium on 'privacy', 'domesticity', and the emotional intimacy between family members. The distance between sexual ideals and actual sexual practices were brought into the open in the 1860s, through the debate on the Contagious Diseases Acts. These Acts, introduced in 1864, 1866 and 1869, were intended to check the spread of venereal disease among enlisted men, and the regulations were applied to eighteen garrison towns and ports. The arbitrary definition of what constituted a 'common prostitute', the humiliating procedures of medical examination, and the double standards involved in the total disregard of the male side of the problem, all of this led to the formation of the Ladies' National Association in 1869, under the leadership of Josephine Butler, and to the successful campaign for the repeal of the Contagious Diseases Acts.

As pointed out by Judith R. Walkowitz,[16] the debate over these Acts highlighted the increasingly interventionist stance of Victorian society in the matter of sexuality, the 'technology of power' involved in the medico-legal regulation of sexual practices.[17] From a feminist point of view, Walkowitz argues, the success of the repeal campaign was an ambiguous one. On the one hand the public visibility of the 'New Woman' and the focus on double standards in sexual matters were indications of real progress. On the other, the campaign was essentially based on the assumption that women were pure, spiritual creatures who needed protection from 'carnal' and promiscuous men. There was no positive assertion of female sexuality, women being still seen as part of the private sphere of the nuclear family, separate from the public sphere of male endeavour (and promiscuity).

From the gentlemanly point of view, things looked a bit different. Sexually speaking, gentlemen could be divided into two categories: married and promiscuous (with prostitutes or others), and bachelor and promiscuous (with prostitutes or others). As Girouard argues,

> The massed ranks of gentlemanly Victorian and Edwardian bachelors were partly the result of social conventions which made it difficult for those of modest income to find wives of their own class; but they were also the result of gentlemen so conditioned by their upbringing that they were as incapable of making contact with a woman as with a working man.[18]

As pointed out by Foucault in his *History of Sexuality*, the (pre-Freudian) coupling of the discourse of sexuality and the discourse of science into a 'scientia sexualis' meant a wholly new and disconcerting view of sexual 'transgression' or 'sin'. The Christian view of sin was basically functional. Man was composed of both good and bad, and one should try to develop the good parts and keep the bad parts in check. The new paradigm of sexual science however, as it developed throughout the nineteenth century, was based on wholly different concepts: the socio-medical ones of health/normality vs. disease/perversion. Sin, in this view, was no longer something you did, but something you 'were', as part of a whole range of scientifically 'explained' perversions, malfunctions or aberrations.

In this sense, as John Fowles puts it in *The French Lieutenant's Woman, Dr Jekyll and Mr Hyde* is indeed 'the best guidebook to the age'. Within this narrow universe of bachelor gentlemen of the professional class, the emerging medico-legal discourse of sexual science is at odds with the 'sub-Christian'[19] residual ethos of the gentleman. The notion of 'sin' as a matter of conduct is literally being 'tested', by scientific experiment, against the idea of sin as a biochemical aberration beyond the influence of human volition. The ambiguity of Jekyll's confession testifies to the unresolved nature of the conflict, the vacillation between repulsion and attraction:

> Men have before hired bravos to transact their crimes, while their own person and reputation sat under shelter. I was the first that ever did so for his pleasures. I was the first that could thus plod in the public eye with a load of genial respectability, and in a moment, like a schoolboy, strip off these lendings and spring headlong into the sea of liberty. (p. 86)

The enormous increase in the production of pornography in this period is a parallel indication of the attractiveness of 'vicarious pleasures', the need to find some sort of compromise between the unfulfilled sexual needs of bachelorhood (or its sexual equivalent in marriage), fuelled as they were by the increased visibility of the 'sin' of the urban environment, and the imperatives of Victorian respectability.

Confessions and investigations

It is apparent to anyone looking into late Victorian masculine romance that two modes of expression predominate: the *confession* and the *investigation*. Both modes pose as not being 'literary' at all. They claim to be without art or artifice, without the aura of the author. Instead, authenticity is what is suggested, the real thing. In the first of four famous examples R.L. Stevenson's *The Strange Case of Dr Jekyll and Mr Hyde* (1886) combines the 'case history' of Jekyll/Hyde with the confessions, i.e. letters, of Dr Lanyon and Dr Jekyll, to be read after they have died.

Arthur Conan Doyle's *The Sign of Four* (1890), the second of the Sherlock Holmes stories, is an account of an investigation, plus the 'confession' of Jonathan Small, the criminal, after he has been apprehended. Conan Doyle actually effaces himself to the extent of presenting Dr Watson as the chronicler of his and Holmes' adventures. Their discussion of the merits of Watson's 'brochure with the somewhat fantastic title of "A Study in Scarlet"', (Doyle's first Sherlock Holmes novel), is an indication of Doyle's role distribution between the two, within the parameters of masculine romance:

> 'I glanced over it,' said he [Holmes]. 'Honestly, I cannot congratulate you upon it. Detection is, or ought to be, an exact science, and should be treated in the same cold and unemotional manner. You have attempted to tinge it with romanticism, which produces much the same effect as if you worked a love-story or an elopement into the fifth proposition of Euclid.'
> 'But the romance was there,' I [Watson] remonstrated. 'I could not tamper with the facts.'
>
> (*The Sign of Four*, p. 15)

Doyle was commissioned to write *The Sign of Four* in 1890 at a dinner with the representative of the American *Lippincott's Magazine*. Dining with them was another masculine romancer of the

1890s, Oscar Wilde, and the work he was commissioned to do was *The Picture of Dorian Gray*, which was published the following year.

In spite of all the differences of style and structure between *The Picture of Dorian Gray* and the Sherlock Holmes stories, the postures and the philosophies of Sir Henry Wotton and Holmes are curiously alike. Sir Henry's 'heavy opium-tainted cigarette' parallels Holmes' addiction to morphine and cocaine. Similarly, Lord Henry's 'scientific' attitude to his 'investigations' echoes that of Holmes:

> He had always been enthralled by the methods of natural science, but the ordinary subject-matter of that science had seemed to him trivial and of no import. And so he had begun by vivisecting himself, as he had ended by vivisecting others. Human life—that appeared to him the one thing worth investigating.
> (*The Picture of Dorian Gray*, p. 66)

Fourthly, as an extreme example of the confessional/investigative mode of narration within late Victorian masculine romance, there is Bram Stoker's *Dracula* from 1897. In *Dracula* there is no authorial voice whatsoever; it is simply a chronological organization of the letters, diaries, journals, including even the transcript of a 'phonograph diary', of four different people. These 'documents', read consecutively, chronicle the horrifying experience the four characters go through with Count Dracula and his cohorts, as well as the process of investigating and tracking down the vampires.

Masculine romance and the loss of confidence

As Weiner suggests in *English Culture and the Decline of the Industrial Spirit*, there is a marked loss of cultural confidence in late Victorian society, and an 'elevation of past over present', which is in contrast to the previous generation. It is my contention that this is equally true when we look at the changing conceptions of what constitutes male behaviour, at representations of masculinity.

Compare the male-female encounters of an early nineteenth-century romance like Walter Scott's *Rob Roy* (1817) and those of Stevenson, Haggard, Doyle or Stoker, and one is struck by at least two ways in which they differ: first (as pointed out by Doyle) there is a marked decline in the overall 'female interest', in favour of the male-male encounter; second, whereas there is in Scott (as in Austen) a relish in describing male and female as equals, at least psychologically, in late Victorian masculine romance 'the female interest' is either absent, *or* described as something threatening or demoniacal, *or* idealized to the point of nausea.

Dr Jekyll and Mr Hyde is a good example of the significant absence of 'the female interest'. *Dracula* offers a striking example of the notion of the threatening female: Lucy Westenra, the sweet (but perhaps too passionate) girl turned vampire, now tracked down by her three former suitors:

> Lucy Westenra, but yet how changed. The sweetness was turned into adamantine, heartless cruelty, and the purity to voluptuous wantonness ... When Lucy—I call the thing that was before us Lucy because it bore her shape—saw us she drew back with an angry snarl, such as a cat gives when taken unawares; then her eyes ranged over us. Lucy's eyes in form and colour, but Lucy's eyes unclean and full of hell-fire, instead of the pure, gentle orbs we knew. At that moment the remnant of my love passed into hate and loathing; had she then to be killed, I could have done it with savage delight. (p. 190)

Conan Doyle is mainly noted for his absence of 'female interest', but in *The Sign of Four*, Watson's anaemic romance with Miss Morstan forms an (unconvincing) 'damsel in distress' subplot, the real couple, of course, being Watson and Holmes. The following *vignette* tells it all: Watson has placed Miss Morstan in the care of dependable Mrs Forrester, and is now on his way to further adventures. There's no place like home—especially when you're leaving it:

> As we drove away I stole a glance back, and I still seem to see that little group on the step—the two graceful, clinging figures, the half-opened door, the hall-light shining through stained glass, the barometer, and the bright stair-rods. It was soothing to catch even that passing glimpse of a tranquil English home in the midst of the wild dark business which had absorbed us. (p. 62)

Ernest Pontifex, Dr Jekyll, Sherlock Holmes, etc., this catalogue of problematic middle-aged bachelor gentlemen maps the late Victorian self-image of a beleaguered, defensive sense of masculinity. The map is incomplete without the reaction formations of Kipling's strutting Jingoist, or the sexually ambiguous Wildean dandy; but the main type is continued in John Buchan's anodyne Richard Hannay (nominally married, but fictionally speaking a true bachelor gentleman).

The 'Great' War killed off the (bachelor) gentleman. Not that he disappeared altogether as a social point of reference, but, after 1918 the ideal of the gentleman had ceased to exist as a major social force. Characters like Sayer's Peter Wimsey or 'Sapper's Bulldog Drummond testify to the fact that henceforth the fictional representations of the gentleman would inevitably find themselves somewhere between pastiche and parody. Household's aristocratic protagonist in *Rogue Male* (1939) is perhaps the last quixotic embodiment of the nineteenth-century bachelor gentleman.

Gentlemanliness: the invention of tradition

'Nine English traditions out of ten date from the latter half of the nineteenth century', it is said in C.P. Snow's novel *The Masters*.[20] This seemingly frivolous statement is borne out by a whole range of research[21] and given full expression in Eric Hobsbawm and Terence Ranger's *The Invention of Tradition*. As Hobsbawm argues,

> ... in consciously setting itself against tradition and for radical innovation, the nineteenth-century liberal ideology of social change systematically failed to provide for the social and authority ties taken for granted in earlier societies, and created voids which might have to be filled by invented practices. (p. 8)

Among the most important 'inventions' are without doubt the reconstruction of the image of the monarchy[22], the construction of an 'age-old' tradition behind the institution of Parliament, and the invention of the nation state with all its paraphernalia of anthems, flags, and so forth.

One significant aspect of the construction of the nineteenth-century gentleman is the development of games, and of the entire code of sportsmanship.[23] Another one is the construction of 'Englishness'. Dr Watson's use of the word 'English' in his reflection on the virtues of 'a tranquil English home', heavy with rural nostalgia and devoid of geographical reference, testifies to the extent to which the concept of 'England' had become ideologized by the 1890s. Domestically the word connoted anti-urbanism and anti-industrialism. The country squire was the central person to identify with, the village was the place to live. Internationally, Englishness, that is patriotism, consisted in the willingness not only to protect this way of life against foreign invasion, but to extend this way of life to all corners of the globe.

Many accounts of the late Victorian construction of gentlemanliness point to the all-pervasive sense of selfconsiousness, of *mise-en-scène*. From the grotesque Eglinton tournament in 1839, when 2690 ladies and gentlemen in medieval costume had to seek umbrage under their umbrellas against the rain, to the chivalrous Baden-Powell boy scout of 1910, there is a sense of the inorganic and contrived, of a pose self-consciously adopted. The masculine romance of the late Victorian period is part of this pose. As Girouard remarks, 'there were few more dedicated cricketers than J.M. Barrie or Conan Doyle, or country gentlemen than Rider Haggard and John Buchan'.[23]

A final note on popular fiction

Is the masculine romance of the late Victorian period 'popular fiction'? Well, leaving aside the vexed discussion of the definition of 'popular', the question can only be satisfactorily answered by going into the actual *reading*, including the readership, of these novels, which would be difficult, except in a conjectural way.

What this article does suggest, however, is that masculine romance relates to a pervasive sense of unease about gender identities, a 'structure of feeling' (to use Raymond Williams's phrase) spreading far beyond its middle-class origins. Also (and this I haven't gone into), masculine romance relates in a complex way to the massive expansion of popular readership of the period, symptoms of which are the sudden death of the three-volume novel in 1894, and the proliferation of new popular media.

Notes

[1] Cf. Raymond Williams's essay on D.H. Lawrence in *Culture and Society*, (London, 1958).

[2] See Freud's famous essay 'Creative Writers and Day-dreaming' (1908).

[3] 'A Gossip on Romance', *Longman's Magazine*, i, (1882–3), pp.69–79.

[4] Cf. J–F. Lyotard's account of the pragmatics of popular narrative in *La Condition Postmoderne* (Paris, 1979).

[5] For a rich study of the social construction of 'taste' see Pierre Bourdieu, *Distinction* (London, 1984).

[6] 'Natural Boundaries: The Social Function of Popular Fiction', *Red Letters* 7.

[7] *The National Review*, 14, (January 1890), pp. 646–57.

[8] See e.g. P. Keating, ed., *Into Unknown England 1866–1913* (Glasgow, 1976).

[9] 'Origins of the Present Crisis', *New Left Review*, no. 23 (January-February 1964), p. 31.

[10] Martin J. Wiener, *English Culture and the Decline of the Industrial Spirit 1850–1980* (Cambridge, 1981).

[11] Philip Mason, *The English Gentleman: The Rise and Fall of an Ideal* (London, 1982).

[12] Mason (1982), p. 161.

[13] Wiener (1981), p. 16.

[14] Wiener (1981), p. 69.

[15] Edward Shorter, *The Making of the Modern Family* (Glasgow, 1975).

[16] Judith R. Walkowitz, *Prostitution and Victorian Society* (Cambridge, 1980).

[17] Cf. Michel Foucault, *The History of Sexuality*, vol. 1 (New York, 1980).

[18] Mark Girouard, *The Return to Camelot: Chivalry and the English Gentleman* (London, 1981), p. 270.

[19] Mason (1982), p. 219.

[20] Called to my attention by Wiener (1981), p. 11.

[21] E.g. Wiener (1981), Girouard (1981) and Hugh A. MacDougall, *Racial Myth in English History* (Montreal, 1982).

[22] See David Cannadine, 'The British Monarchy, c. 1820–1977' in E. Hobsbawm and T. Ranger (eds), *The Invention of Tradition* (Cambridge, 1983).

[23] Girouard (1981), p. 269.

Editions used

Oscar Wilde, *The Picture of Dorian Gray* (Harmondsworth, 1984)
R.L. Stevenson, *Dr Jekyll and Mr Hyde and Other Stories* (Harmondsworth, 1984)
Bram Stoker, *Dracula* (London, 1970)
Arthur Conan Doyle, *The Sign of Four* (John Murray and Jonathan Cape, London, 1974)

'Great Expectations': Masculinity and Modernity

CAROLYN BROWN

Just as masculinity seems to dominate the world, so too does modernity seem the only mode of existing. As an atmosphere, a whole culture, it makes it difficult to become even dimly aware of the conceptual boundaries which construct and circumscribe our languages, our thoughts. Both, it seems, engage in the masquerade of universality, posing as the only mode of orientation to the world.

And yet what are these words? To what do they refer? How closely are they entwined? Are they, within our history, so intimately enmeshed as to constitute the same phenomenon? Can we indeed undo these universalities to reveal them as partial, as historical and discursive constructs, without setting up new universalities?

In this essay I will attempt to look at masculinity and modernity as motifs in Charles Dickens's *Great Expectations*. While my discussion will rely upon these as specific strands in the problem of 'identity', I would like also to locate them as general phenomena. The perspective of 'post-modernism' offers a position, however fictional, which refuses the nostalgia usually present in critiques of 'modernity' and in refusing this nostalgia permits a critique of 'masculinity'.

Jürgen Habermas has brought to English readers' attention the work of Hans Robert Jauss on the term 'modern' which dates the word from its Latin form 'modernus' in the late fifth century. Thereafter,

> ... the term 'modern' appeared and reappeared exactly during those periods in Europe when the consciousness of a new epoch formed itself through a renewed relationship to the ancients—whenever, moreover, antiquity was considered to be a model to be recovered through some kind of imitation.

Habermas argues that a significant shift took place in the early nineteenth century, which opposed an idealized Middle Ages to the antique ideals of the classicists. During the course of the nineteenth century, this became an aesthetic modernity 'that radicalized consciousness of modernity and freed it from all specific historical ties'.[1]

Craig Owens in an interesting essay has considered the construction of discourse in dominance to the masculine, arguing that

> It is precisely at the legislative frontier between what can be represented and what cannot that the postmodernist operation is being staged—not in order to transcend representation, but in order to expose that system of power that authorizes certain representations while blocking, prohibiting or invalidating others. Among those prohibited from Western representation, whose representations are denied all legitimacy, are women. Excluded from representation by its very structure, they return within it as a figure for—a representation of—the unrepresentable (Nature, Truth, the Sublime, etc.). This prohibition bears primarily on women as the subject, and rarely as the object of representation, for there is certainly no shortage of images *of* women.[2]

Together, these versions indicate a model of 'modernity' which is decentered, yet constructed in dominance to, overdetermined by, the masculine. 'Modernity' and 'masculinity' are fragmented, historically structured and historically dominant.

In this essay, I am interested in these aspects of our history as constructing identities, and in enabling those identities to be written, in constructing a 'speaking subject'. *Great Expectations* is an account of development of identity in a 'modern' world, but also (to me) an extraordinarily masculine world. In this text, women are present only to be incorporated into men, to be destroyed, or as narcissistic reflections. Insofar as Pip's development of identity can proceed beyond an enclosed narcissism, it operates primarily within a masculine homosocial world, within the dynamics of power of that world, and within relations of love which occur within those relations of power. This construction is geo-historically specific, and an essential component is the reviewing of traditional narratives at a time of change and transformation.

I will elaborate further on this complex formulation in the course of this essay, but I wish first to consider the specifics of English 'modernity' through two recent American texts. Marshall Berman's *All That is Solid Melts into Air* takes its title from 'The Manifesto of the Communist Party', where Marx wrote of the 'constant revolutionizing of production, uninterrupted disturbance of all social conditions, everlasting uncertainty and agitation'. This is perceived by Berman as the essence of the modern, and his celebration of modernity through selected modernist texts excludes Dickens, and, excepting the Crystal Palace, Britain. Berman's perspective operates as it were negatively upon the subject of this essay. Martin J. Wiener opens his book *English Culture and The Decline of The Industrial Spirit* by observing that 'the leading problem of modern British history is the explanation of economic decline'. The Crystal Palace, which Berman celebrates as 'the most visionary and adventurous building of the whole nineteenth century ... [a] lyrical expression of the potentialities of an industrial age' (p. 237) appears now as the beginning of the end of English modernity, of English modernism, of English hegemony. Wiener points out that 'planted within the Great Exhibition itself was a core of cultural opposition, represented by Augustus Pugin's Medieval Court' (p. 28). English bourgeois culture turned to the construction of a faked and forged history.[3]

Wiener argues that Dickens (whose writings have served as the basis of much of our theme-park history) apparently opposed the nostalgia for 'those infernally and damnably good old times' (p. 33), yet in later years moved 'towards an affirmation of a gentlemanly ideal ... purged of its associations with class and social ambition' (cited p. 35). Clearly, the 'gentleman ideal' is by no means dissociated from class and social ambition. Rather, in *Great Expectations* it points to a crucial moment of development of 'Englishness', as an identity based upon the 'gentlemanly ideal' formed within the intersection of historically located masculinities and modernities.[4]

This identity was not 'imposed' in any simple way but was actively sought after as a mode of negotiating cultural transformations. Patrick Wright has recently drawn attention to Agnes Heller's formulation of the problem of identity in modernity. He cites from *A Theory of Feelings* Heller's observation that

> Bourgeois society is the first 'pure' society; natural or blood kinship no longer determines the path of the individual. At the same time it is a dynamic society, and increasingly so; the tasks to be dealt with change continually from the point of view of every stratum and class, often even within the space of a generation. With the disintegration of community ties the individual becomes an 'accidental' individual [his class—or stratum]—is of accidental character but, at the same time he becomes a free individual as well, at least potentially.[5]

Using *Great Expectations* as a 'memory which flashes up at a moment of danger', I would argue that the 'gentlemanly ideal', dislodged from a feudal location with the changes of English society, was not merely made available as a model for the rising bourgeoisie, but rather, disseminated through the proliferating products of the press, moved into the most unlikely places, operating within the reformation of English capitalism as it demanded competent clerical-managerial labour in its imperialist operations.[6] Moreover, propagated through the English educational system it continues as an 'ideal', as a basis from which to write, to speak, to be heard.

The world of *Great Expectations* is in a process of rapid social and textual transformation. Edward Said has used the Hamlet scene in *Great Expectations* to demonstrate Derrida's points concerning the myth of presence in Western culture. I have not the space here to rehearse fully Said's excellent analysis of this scene, but what concerns us is the point that

> if we say that *Hamlet* as Shakespeare wrote it is at the centre or origin of the whole episode, then what Dickens gives us is a comically literal account of the centre not only unable to hold, but *being* unable to hold, producing instead a number of new, devastatingly eccentric multiples of the play.[7]

Said demonstrates that the philosophic ideas of Jacques Derrida concerning 'voice, presence, and metaphysical "origins"' are assumed in a most unphilosophic way by Dickens; and if we consider the wonderful *bricolage* which is Shakespeare's *Hamlet* we have evidence that the posing of open, multi-referential texts against bourgeois notions of unified, realist, texts, or subjects, enables us to abandon a morality of the text, the subject, to consider its textuality, its historicity.

Apparently paradoxically, the world in which writing acquires such a reality, in which identity becomes so problematic, is a world of increasing organization, increasing regulation.[8] From the beginning to the end of the novel, it is made clear what 'identity' means to Magwitch, who is a victim of the growing state apparatus of control and surveillance.

While the efforts of the State to locate and identify its individuals is but one aspect of the question of identity, of subjectivity, which is present in *Great Expectations* it is nonetheless vitally important. For it seems that in this Dickensian world, there is very little certainty of identity as an essential attribute, somehow tagged by a legal label. Rather identity is entangled within the operations of the legal system, within the operations of writing, from its outset. If we turn to Pip's relationship with Magwitch the matter will become clearer.

> 'I do not even know' said I, speaking low as he took his seat at the table, 'by what name to call you. I have given out that you are my uncle.'
> 'That's it, dear boy! Call me uncle.'
> 'You assumed some name, I suppose, on board ship?'
> 'Yes, dear boy. I took the name of Provis.'
> 'Do you mean to keep that name?'
> 'Why, yes, dear boy, it's as good as another—unless you'd like another.'
> 'What is your real name?' I asked him in a whisper.
> 'Magwitch,' he answered in the same tone: 'chrisen'd Abel.'
> 'What were you brought up to be?'
> 'A warmint, dear boy.'
> He answered quite seriously, and used the word as if it denoted some profession.
> (*Great Expectations*, p. 345)

For Magwitch, recognition in London, identification as the same (*idem*), convicted, person, can only bring death on the gibbet. His refuge is in a *provis*-ional name, by which he can function in society (and to which he is indifferent) without incurring the penalty of the Law, Death, which will stop the fluctutation of identity. Yet, in fixing the identity finally, Death also brings annihilation.

The organization and regulation of society depends upon making people accountable for their actions, by insisting upon a continuation of identity, a retention of a name, a label, in order to locate potentially mobile and fluid existences. During the eighteenth century, and increasingly in the nineteenth century, an immense apparatus is constructed to fix, locate, and stabilize the young and mobile population brought forth by the social and economic changes. Births, deaths, and marriages must be registered. It becomes essential to belong to a certain geo-political unit, a certain nation-state. Existences become regulated, according to a system which becomes increasingly homogenized, in order to control an increasingly heterogeneous social body.

The world of *Great Expectations* is a transitional world. Pip moves between the small local scale of organization in the village in Kent, and the vast global system which radiates from London. Yet perhaps to put it like this is to overstate the opposition. For the world of *Great*

Expectations, in the village almost as much as the city, is not only extraordinarily violent, but abounds in orphans, in non-existent or inadequate parenting. Pip has been raised by his sister, Mrs Joe, whose husband is no candidate for the role of surrogate patriarch.[9] Yet Pip's environment is stable compared to the account which Jaggers (the intermediary between the regulatory apparatus and those it desires to regulate) gives of the state of children in the early nineteenth century. It is an account of anarchy. '" . . . all he saw of children, was, their being generated in great numbers for certain destruction . . . being imprisoned, whipped, transported, neglected, cast out, . . . and growing up to be hanged."' (pp. 424–425).

Great Expectations is told by the adult. It is a *bildungsroman* which seems to lead nowhere, but to enable this narrative to be recounted, this identity to be fixed and located. For, as the developing nineteenth-century state organizes identity, 'identity' comes to be problematic to the individual subject. The mobility of existences places considerable stress upon subjectivity: in a dis-continuous existence, continuities become necessary. Narcissism (for what form can be more narcissistic than the autobiography?) becomes a necessary device for survival. It becomes essential to write a 'self', to construct an order from the chaos, to locate oneself in some way within the ordering of power.

Great Expectations opens with the presentation of Pip in the graveyard, viewing his family. He names himself first. He is 'Pip'; he has acquired this name through his inability to speak his father's name which he has been given. He shares his father's name, even as he differentiates himself from it. This self-naming, this differentiation, has been accepted by those who surround him. Pip's father's name is presented in relation to Pip, not as quoted from the tombstone, unlike his mother's name. 'Also Georgina, his wife' is more central within that first paragraph as a name, than the father's, perhaps as a part of Pip's infancy. 'Also Georgina' is nonetheless defined in relation to her husband, as a supplement to the (assumed but absent) centrality of the father's name at the head of the tombstone.

The moment at which Pip's identity is established, his consciousness assumed, is the moment preceding Magwitch's appearance. This trauma is that which constructs identity, making possible the reviewing of the aquisition of consciousness. The events before the trauma acquire their significance in the light, or the shadow, of the trauma. Pip's account constructs the events thus:

My first most vivid and broad impression of the identity of things, seems to me to have been gained on a memorable raw afternoon towards evening. At such a time I found out for certain, that this bleak place overgrown with nettles was the churchyard; and that Philip Pirrip, late of this parish, and also Georgina wife of the above, were dead and buried; ... and that the low leaden line beyond, was the marshes; and that the distant savage lair from which the wind was rushing, was the sea; and that the small bundle of shivers growing afraid of it all and beginning to cry, was Pip. (pp. 35–36)

The nature of the 'father' who ushers Pip into the Lacanian Symbolic, is that of a *carnivalesque* Patriarch.[10] Using threats of penetration, mutilation, and absorbtion ('... I'll cut your throat!' 'What fat cheeks you ha' got.' 'Darn me if I couldn't eat them.' '... I'll have your heart and liver out') (pp. 36, 37) Magwitch directs Pip against his home, confounding that order. Like the wolf in *Little Red Riding Hood*, like the witches greeting Macbeth, *Mag-witch* is the harbinger of disruption. Threatening the body of the barely established consciousness of the 'small bundle of shivers', he upturns Pip not only physically, but conceptually. Transgressing the small world by bursting in from outside, Magwitch, as anarchy, brings consciousness to Pip, not only as a self, but of all things as a source of fear.

This account of the assumption of consciousness, bears all the marks of the 'agonising transition'[11], but the archetype of the Oedipal family, with a maternal Imaginary, is present in *Great Expectations*, as an 'original' known only by a parodic echoing. 'Also Georgina' occupies the role of mother, but is known only through the writing on her tombstone, which thus confirms her absence. Pip's acquisition of consciousness is a messy, untidy, process, in which writing, divorced from any authentic source, plays an essential part. It is between the 'real' world and the 'textual' world of writing and reading that Pip is formed. It is between reading the inscriptions on the tombstones and the assault by Magwitch that Pip comes to consider his 'self'.

At the end of the first chapter, Pip constructs the world around him in terms of horizontal lines, with two vertical lines, intersecting. One is a guide for voyagers, the other a sign of the law:

The marshes were just a long black horizontal line then, as I stopped to look after him; and the river was just another horizontal line, not nearly so broad nor yet so black. and the sky was just a

MASCULINITY AND MODERNITY

row of long angry red lines and dense black lines intermixed. On the edge of the river I could faintly make out the only two black things in all the prospect that seemed to be standing upright; one of these was the beacon by which the sailors steered—like an unhooped cask upon a pole—an ugly thing when you were near it; the other a gibbet, with some chains hanging to it which had once held a pirate. (p. 39)

This typographical world in which Pip exists, exhibits signs of other worlds, other existences, but also of danger, of death. These signal the inhospitable, hostile world in which an 'identity', some stable ensemble must be inscribed.

Following the narration of his encounter with Magwitch and the Law, Pip relates his experiences in the acquisition of literacy at the evening school kept by Mr Wopsle's great-aunt, assisted by her granddaughter, Biddy. Just as the landscape has appeared as a threatening series of lines, so do letters and numbers appear as physical entities.

Much by my unassisted self, and more by the help of Biddy than of Mr Wopsle's great-aunt, I struggled through the alphabet as if it had been a bramble-bush; getting considerably worried and scratched by every letter. After that, I fell among those thieves, the nine figures, who seemed every evening to do something new to disguise themselves and baffle recognition. But, at last I began, in a purblind groping way to read, write and cipher, on the very smallest scale. (p. 75)

The devices of representation have a physical presence and importance, and their promiscuous intermingling 'organizes' Pip's perception of himself and the world. It is an organization of scraps of inaccurate fragments. Of his reading of the family tombstones Pip recalls that 'my construction even of their simple meaning was not very correct' and that his understanding of the Catechism as a declaration to ' "walk in the same all the days of my life", laid me under an obligation always to go through the village from our house in one particular direction' (p. 73). This is not a simple account of childish incomprehension, for it is made clear that similar states of ignorance exist in the entire village, all of whom, it seems, share the 'Educational scheme' of Mr Wopsle's great-aunt. Narrative, as a coherent linear form, does not organize this world: rather there is a jumble of garbled odds and ends, an ensemble of the flotsam and jetsam of discourse. It is not only that the realm of writing manifests itself in fragments, it is also that the reading, the meaning that these acquire, are various and unpredictable. Nevertheless they are ordered in some way, and desires are ushered into existence, and take effect on the real world. Pip writes his first letter to Joe, a year after his encounter with Magwitch. It is a wonderfully graphic piece of writing setting out his desires to teach Joe, to be apprenticed to him, to be close to him. Through the distance provided by writing, Pip 'speaks' his desires, although 'there was no indispensable necessity for my communicating with Joe by letter, inasmuch as he sat beside me and we were alone' (p. 75).

Writing connects Pip to his parents, separates him from his sister, and permits the declaration of love for Joe. It acquires a reality in the child's life, and directs him to a desire of being the Prince to the Sleeping Beauty hidden behind those thickets of discourse. Thus, in this reading, Pip's first and indeed crucial action is the acquisition of literacy, which pre-dates his encounter with Magwitch, with Satis House, yet is fixed and reinforced by those encounters.

I have noted the absence of a maternal figure for Pip. The discovery of the masculine world is an essential aspect of the narrative. It is Magwitch, not Miss Haversham who is the fairy godmother to this Cinderella; and, as with the Miss Haversham–Estella relationship, it is quite clear what this relationship is based upon. Pip's filial position is purchased by the convict's money, and Pip is living out the convict's carefully nurtured fantasies of revenge:

> 'And then, dear boy, it was a recompense to me, look'ee here, to know in secret that I was making a gentleman. The blood horses of them colonists might fling up the dust over me as I was walking; what do I say? I says to myself, "I'm making a better gentleman nor *you*'ll ever be!" When one of . . . I says to myself, "If I ain't a gentleman, nor yet ain't got no learning, I'm the owner of such . . . a bought-up London gentleman?"' (p. 339)

Perhaps it is a mark of how endemic are the expectations that one can buy vicarious satisfaction through another, that Pip's abhorrence, dread, and repugnance of the source of his great expectations have been termed 'snobbish'. For not only is it made clear that it is a network of criminality and capitalism in which he exists (rather than Miss Haversham's tastefully unstated *rentier* income), but that he is the product of these forces, that his desires for gentility have been shared by Magwitch. He is the product of Magwitch's desires, and is possessed by him.

Magwitch's displaced desires for gentility make it clear that Pip's wishes are not an isolated and eccentric desire, but a widespread social phenomenon: Magwitch's reasons are made clear, and his demonstration that it is money which buys the 'character' of a gentleman is borne out. Ironically, Pip's 'gentlemanly' refusal of Magwitch's money is backed up by the State which sequesters Magwitch's money as it kills him.

Pip's collapse following Magwitch's death results in a breakdown of identity:

> That I had a fever and was avoided, that I suffered greatly, that I often lost my reason, that the time seemed interminable, that I confounded impossible existences with my own identity; that I was a brick in the house wall, and yet entreating to be released from the giddy place where the builders had set me; that I was a steel beam of a vast engine, clashing and whirling over a gulf, and yet that I implored in my own person to have the engine stopped, and my part in it hammered off; that I passed through these phases of disease, I know of my own remembrance, and did in some sort know it at the time. That I sometimes struggled with real people, in the belief that they were murderers, and that I would all at once comprehend that they meant to do me good, and would then sink exhausted into their arms, and suffer them to lay me down, I also knew at the time. But, above all, I knew that there was a constant tendency in all these people—who when I was very ill, would present all kinds of extraordinary transformations of the human face, and would be much dilated in size—above all, I say, I knew that there was an extraordinary tendency in all these people to settle down in the likeness of Joe. (pp. 471–2)

Pip is rescued from the nightmare of anonymity and confusion by Joe, who rescues him from absorbtion in a terrifying industrial psychic world, where 'real people' are assumed to be murderers. Joe becomes, in the words of Dickens's draft, a ministering angel; the vision of Joe is a loving reconciliation to the world, a rebirth, with Magwitch eliminated. It is a touching relationship.[12] Joe functions in the novel as the embodiment of 'home', 'sanctifying' what is otherwise a bleak, inhospitable, unpleasant and violent community. Joe provides the point at which the loss of the ties of childhood, of community, is rendered mythical. Joe sanctifies masculinity.

I have noted that Pip's casting of himself in the role of Miss

Haversham's Cinderella turned Prince to Estella's Sleeping Beauty is a mistaken narrative, one which attributes a power of transformation to women when they in the 'real' story have none. Moreover, Miss Haversham bears an uncanny resemblance to Also Georgina:

> Once, I had been taken to see some ghastly waxwork at the Fair, ... Once, I had been taken to one of our old marsh churches to see a skeleton in the ashes of a rich dress, ... Now, waxwork and skeleton seemed to have dark eyes that looked out at me. (p. 88)

> ... I began to understand that everything in the room had stopped ... a long time ago ... Without this arrest of everything, this standing still of pale decayed objects, not even the withered bridal dress on the collapsed form could have looked so like grave-clothes, or the long veil so like a shroud. So she sat, corpse-like, as we played at cards. (pp. 89–90)

This corpse-like maternal phantom lingers throughout the novel, even after a partial and *pre-mortem* cremation. Miss Haversham is not the only woman in the novel to suffer death-in-life. The vigorous Mrs Joe is struck down by Orlick with Magwitch's leg-iron; Estella's once murderous mother, whom Pip first sees after going to *Macbeth*, is kept well under control by Jaggers. Through the apparently naive and gentlemanly Pip, *Great Expectations* creates a world in which only the biddable Biddy, and the sweet betrotheds of Wemmick and Herbert can survive.

The sexual politics of Estella's upbringing are explained to Pip by Herbert. She is ' "hard and haughty and capricious to the last degree, and has been brought up by Miss Haversham to wreak revenge on all the male sex." ' (p. 200). Estella's role as guerilla in the gender war meets with failure; she is made to marry the brutal Bentley Drummle, 'who ... used her with great cruelty' (p. 492). Estella resembles those narcissistic women described by Freud as being particularly attractive to men. The normal male, according to Freud (*On Narcissism*) displays 'complete object-love of the attachment type', which 'displays the marked sexual overvaluation which ... corresponds to a transference of (the original) narcissism to the sexual object.' The object choice is the narcissistic woman who takes herself as object. Freud elaborates:

> The importance of this type of woman for the erotic life of mankind is to be rated very high ... The great charm of narcissis-

tic women has, however, its reverse side; a large part of the lover's dissatisfaction, of his doubts of the woman's love, of his complaints of her enigmatic nature, has its root in this incongruity between the types of object choice.

This description traces the terrain of Pip's experiences, of his desires. Constructed as a reflection of 'normal' masculine narcissism, Estella is denied any autonomy. Pip's extraordinary declarations, disperse and incorporate her at the same time.

> '... You are part of my existence, part of myself. You have been in every line I have ever read, since I first came here, the rough common boy whose poor heart you wounded even then. You have been in every prospect I have ever seen since—on the river, on the sails of the ships, on the marshes, in the clouds, in the sea, in the streets. You have been the embodiment of every graceful fancy that my mind has ever been acquainted with ... Estella, to the last hour of my life, you cannot choose but remain part of my character, part of the little good in me, part of the evil.'
> (*Great Expectations*. p. 378.)

Arguably, Pip's search for Estella's true identity, as daughter of the Magwitches, as well as the adopted daughter of the phantom bride, can be seen as a displaced search for his own identity. That Magwitch is Pip's 'second father' conjures up that wisp of incest so beloved by the Gothic, and also incorporates Estella with Pip. It would seem that the desires for gentility, apparently unleashed by Satis House, are nothing more than a reflection back from the enigma of woman, which can yet be blamed upon the reflecting surface.

Great Expectations, then, presents the formation of an identity of a 'gentleman', or rather of a clerk, a businessman, who will go abroad to work 'for profits', although, we are assured that the firm was 'not in a grand way of business, but we had a good name' (p. 489). This identity is located at the period of British ascendency over the globe. It is constructed in a network of the movements of the growing legal system, the movements of expanding capitalism, the movements of a proliferating writing of fragmentary narratives, dislocated from their existence in traditional and stable settings. In the interstices of these systems, it seems that 'identity' is an uncertain matter: yet it takes, for Pip and for Magwitch, the form of desiring to acquire the characteristics of the dominant class, which then come into play in quite different formations.

I have made use in this essay of *Great Expectations* in order to attempt to draw out some points which, while hardly novel, are worth repeating.[13] *Great Expectations*' status, not only as literary 'classic' but also as a children's book, its presence in our culture, rendered this attempt, for me at any rate, particularly interesting. It is a disconcerting tale. While Pip may grow to reconcile his gentlemanly ideal to his employment in the world of commerce—and in this sense it is an expression of that rising sector of finance capital, which will become of increasing importance in the British economy—we should observe the exclusions, and prohibitions within this development. (During the nineteenth century, and continuing now, a regime of education is developed which is far more carefully controlled than Pip's, but also building upon this 'ideal' masculine world.) Wiener notes that the English public school had 'become by the end of Victoria's reign the shared formative experience of most members of the English elite (p. 16). The gentlemanly ideal was also applied to girls' schools, and it is not insignificant that Radclyffe Hall in constructing the paragon lesbian-novelist for *The Well of Loneliness* made 'Stephen' into the gentlemanly ideal, complete with fencing skills and silk shirts. Perhaps neither class nor gender was any substantial impediment in accepting the mould, which operates as an entry point into an active subjectivity: so long as either discrepancy could be repudiated in the embracing of the image of the dominant class, in order to claim a share in its privileges, which included, not least, the right to speak.

Notes

[1] J. Habermas, 'Modernity—an Incomplete Project', in *Postmodern Culture*, ed. Hal Foster (London, 1985), pp. 3–4.

[2] C. Owens, 'Feminists and Postmodernism', in *Postmodern Culture*, p. 59.

[3] M. Berman, *All That is Solid Melts into Air* (New York, 1981); M. J. Wiener, *English Culture and the Decline of the Industrial Spirit* (Cambridge, 1981).

[4] The complexity of this historical phenomenon is illustrated by Stuart Hall, who takes the statement 'an Englishman's home is his castle' and notes that although it has 'acquired the status of eternal proverbial English wisdom' it is in fact the product of an immensely complex and specific history. Hall locates this within the emergence of liberalism as English common

MASCULINITY AND MODERNITY

sense. 'The whole liberal tradition of the "free born Englishman" and his rights and the whole history of the emergence of "civil society" in the seventeenth and eighteenth centuries is already inscribed in that proverbial statement'. S. Hall, 'Variants of liberalism', in J. Donald and S. Hall, eds, *Politics and Ideology* (Milton Keynes, 1986).

[5] P. Wright, *Living in an Old Country* (London, 1985), p. 13. Whether 'identity' became obviously 'problematic' for everyone at this time is difficult to determine. My suggestion here is that 'the gentlemanly ideal' operates as a 'fictional' attempt at resolution, which both claims the privileges of that class (as part of the democratization of the liberal property-based order) and yet as *simulacrum* reinforces that class order.

[6] The phrase is from W. Benjamin, 'Theses on the Philosophy of History', in H. Arendt, ed., *Illuminations* (London, 1982), p. 257. Raymond Williams observes that the eleven million people in the British mainland at the end of the eighteenth century had doubled by the middle of the nineteenth century. He estimates that four or five million people had some degree of literacy by the end of the eighteenth century: by 1840 some twelve million, by 1870 more than twenty million. R. Williams, 'Notes on English Prose', in *Writing in Society* (London, n.d.), pp.70–1.

[7] E. Said, 'Criticism between Culture and System' in his *The World, The Text and the Critic* (London, 1984), pp. 198–9.

[8] This construction of history draws upon the work of Michel Foucault, especially in his *Discipline and Punish* (London, 1977) and *The History of Sexuality, Volume One* (New York, 1978), and Jacques Donzelot's *The Policing of Families* (London, 1980). Foucault's argument concerning bio-power is particularly relevant here:

> if the development of the great instruments of the state, as *institutions* of power, ensured the maintenance of production relations, the rudiments of anatamo- and bio-politics, created in the eighteenth century as *techniques* of power present at every level of the social body and utilized by very diverse institutions (the family and the army, schools, and the police, individual medicine, and the administration of collective bodies) operated in the sphere of economic processes, their development, and the forces working to sustain them. They also acted as factors of segregation and social hierarchization, exerting their influence on the respective forces of both these movements, guaranteeing relations of domination and effects of hegemony.

Foucault, *History of Sexuality*, p. 141.

[9] Pip's home is one in which the classic patriarchal arrangement is reversed. Mrs Joe might have had to adopt her husband's name but she is Pip's 'all-powerful sister' (p. 46), who has brought him up 'by hand': 'having at that time to find out for myself what the expression meant, and knowing her to have a hard and heavy hand, and to be much in the habit of laying it upon her husband as well as upon me, I supposed that Joe Gargery and I were both brought up by hand' (p. 39).

[10] I use these terms somewhat 'against the grain', but they serve to reinforce the connection between language and power, between an order constructed in dominance to the masculine and the acquistion of identity, which I am concerned to elaborate here. Toril Moi summarizes the formulation thus:

> The Imaginary and Symbolic Order constitute one of the most fundamental sets of related terms in Lacanian theory . . . The Imaginary corresponds to the pre-Oedipal period when the child believes itself to be a part of the mother, and perceives no separation between itself and the world. In the Imaginary there is no difference and no absence, only identity and presence. The Oedipal crisis represents the entry into the Symbolic Order. This entry is also linked to the acquisitions of language.

(Toril Moi, *Sexual/Textual Politics*, London, 1985, p. 99). Bakhtin's notion of the *carnivalesque* incorporates the idea of an overturning and a parody of the dominant order, but as an ambivalent action which may act as confirmation of that order. See M. Bakhtin, *Rabelais and his World* (Bloomington, 1984).

[11] The phrase is used to great effect by Fredric Jameson, 'Imaginary and Symbolic in Lacan: Marxism, Psychoanalytic Criticism, and the Problem of the Subject', in *Psychoanalysis and Literature*, ed. Shoshana Felman (Baltimore, 1982), p. 360.

[12] For instance: ' "Oh dear good Joe, whom I was so ready to leave and so unthankful to, I see you again, with your broad muscular blacksmith's arm before your eyes, and your broad chest heaving, and your voice dying away. O dear good faithful tender Joe, I feel the loving tremble of your hand upon my arm, as solemnly this day as if it had been the rustle of angel's wings!" ' (p. 168)

[13] They are but an elaboration on work proceeding from Perry Anderson, 'Origins of the Present Crisis', *New Left Review* 23.

Different Starting Points
A view of teaching 'English etc' from Further Education
DEE EDWARDS, DAVID MAUND, JOHN MAYNARD

Sitting in the canteen of a Further Education college, you can watch the whole world go by. Or, if not *quite* the whole world, at least a pretty good local microcosm. You can see engineering students, secretarial students, 'scheme teenagers', people in for the morning to take 'matures' or recreational classes, visiting businessmen on short courses, and some people just come in out of the cold to sit down. Many backgrounds, many expectations . . .

For teachers with 'English' degrees, Further Education has always been a fairly messy area: certainly not about passing on a unified body of knowledge by an agreed method. For instance, the three of us have taught not only traditional (and 'progressive') 'O' and 'A' Level English to sixteen to nineteen year-olds and adults, but also 'English' or 'Communications' to business students, secretaries, nurses, hairdressers, engineers, English-as-a-Second-Language speakers and (once upon a time) apprentices. We've taught evening classes in contemporary literature, 'creative writing', sexual politics . . . The seventies saw Communications 'A' Level (a huge mix, involving some social history, the sociology of the mass media, the psychology of perception, copy-writing), the Youth Opportunities Programme and BTEC (business and technical education courses, which offer to replace 'O' and 'A' Levels as qualifications for such jobs as there are and for higher education). And, more recently, there has been the New Vocationalism in the form of—more cabbalistic acronyms—YTS, CPVE, TVEI and others.[1] There are growing opportunities now for English teachers to move towards 'Media Studies'. And learning packs and distance learning . . . and . . . and . . .

This enormous range of courses (which perhaps we need to call 'English etc' for the moment) makes it difficult to hold to the notion of one standard 'literary' culture. It isn't only the range of courses, it's also the range of backgrounds and the diversity of students on these courses. To try to maintain a unified literary culture in the face of this is to invite defeat and despair—you might end up like Tom Sharpe's Wilt, teaching *Lord of the Flies* and *Sons and Lovers* to 'Gasfitters One' and 'Meat Two', and drowning in cynicism.

In this article we try to pull together some strands in our own teaching experiences. The formal structures of 'English' are changing rapidly in FE, and—where teachers have room to manoeuvre—moves can be made towards versions of 'English' which relate better to students' interests and demands. For instance, the New Vocationalism is dominating a great deal of colleges' work, and so we look at what the role of the English teacher might be. In some ways our methods might be seen as an attempt to put together elements of 'progressive' English teaching and Cultural Studies. From progressive English it might be possible to take some notions of 'starting where the students are', student activity, group work, and even the tricky use of 'experience'. From Cultural Studies we might want to take some of the *range* of 'culture' to be studied (a diversity of writings and visual images, mass media, the sense of audience/users' reactions, whole ways of living and struggling), and also the sense of cultural divisions—most obviously those of class, gender, race, age and geography—which are the ways in which power differences in society are lived out and struggled over. We describe our exploratory moves to break down cultural hierarchies. Finally, we advocate student activity and participation in organizing classes and projects, and discuss problems with this.

'English' has been expanding in terms of content, even at 'A' Level. In the past ten years new versions and possibilities in English 'A' Level have opened up.[2] For example, the AEB's English Syllabus III (660) gives one third of its marks for coursework and an extended essay, books can be taken into the exams, and centres can *choose* (with the approval of a moderator) six texts to study. The scheme, although still tending to revolve around 'close reading and response' in the exam, is allowing for greater flexibility than in the past—including period studies for extended essays, pastiche and even 'theoretical' approaches. Of course, many teachers still find new ways of teaching 'classic' texts inventively, putting them in their historical context, showing the conflicts within them, and encouraging students to explore actively what is involved. However, new syllabuses also allow, and even sometimes encourage centres to choose a wider range of material than the traditional English Literature canon. For example, our own choices have included contemporary writing like Alan Bleasdale's plays, *Boys from the Blackstuff*, Buchi Emecheta's novel, *Second-Class Citizen*, Amrit Wilson's *Finding A Voice: Asian Women in Britain*, Beatrix Campbell's *Wigan Pier Revisited*, and a provocative anthology of mainly modern prose in a variety of genres, *Varieties of Writing*.[3]

Material like this raises all sorts of questions (and some eyebrows). Working on a 'television script' (*Boys from the Blackstuff*), for instance, has been controversial with some traditionalist teachers (whose tone of voice has sometimes seemed to imply '*mere* television script'). The objections have usually been that the finished product is not the work of just one person, and that there are determinations of the medium that require a different kind of work—work on more than 'the text'. Well, we could argue that both points might also apply to *Hamlet*. We might go further and suggest that any 'literature' requires the study of more than just 'the text': also of its conditions of production, its distribution, its use of genre conventions, representations and ideologies, its imagined audience and the responses of real audiences. Perhaps one day an 'A' Level will be able to include all these—whether it be called Language, Literature, Communications, Media Studies or Cultural Studies. Meanwhile, perhaps there are some justifications for looking at Bleasdale's plays even in terms of 'style' and 'content' (side by side with some of the above, albeit gestural as yet). Using highly skilful narrative techniques and vivid idiom, Bleasdale's plays examine complex questions about relationships and identities under stress (caused by unemployment), the uses of humour, the ambivalent face of the Welfare State, notions of 'community', women's positions (although women have a rather low visibility in the plays), and more. Some of these matters are only too accessible to students today, and the plays can generate great energy and interest. Similarly, in an inner city college, debates around contemporary books like *Finding A Voice* and *Second-Class Citizen* have not only cut across race and gender barriers but have led to discussions continuing outside the classroom long after the lesson is over. They have prompted students to continue the process of discovery by actively seeking out books by the same author or by other black or Asian writers (which can be material for extended essays).

However, colleges are involved in more than 'A' Levels. Since James Callaghan began 'The Great Debate' about education, FE English teachers have had to face the challenge of the 'New Vocationalism'. A public 'common sense' seems to have been created that, brought up in too much affluence, working-class school leavers were not being prepared for the 'world of work', their 'natural' destination. Instead they were being given an academic education, unsuitable for their role within the economy and filling their heads with irrelevancies.

Under the Conservative government the Manpower Services Commission has been vastly expanded and funded with comparable largesse. The initials DES in the early eighties became a by-word for ossification and fossilisation, while the initials MSC spawned multiple initials all designed to inculcate a new 'realistic' approach to training a national workforce: YOPS, WEEPS, TOPS.[4] These in turn gave birth to YTS and several smaller sister and brother training schemes, most significantly perhaps the Technical and Vocational Education Initiative, which can start in schools at fourteen. In retaliation, and showing itself capable of giving birth too, the DES has eventually produced the CPVE, the one-year Certificate of Pre-Vocational Education for sixteen-year-olds.

The thinking behind these courses often assumes that young people in the future will have to move from job to job (and spend long periods out of work). Thus, 'flexible' and 'transferable' skills are to be taught, along with positive attitudes, self-presentation, good time-keeping and so on (Work Discipline Across the Curriculum?).

Communications/English teachers are usually thought to have a part to play in these new syllabuses. This part is often expected to be as providers of a *medium*, as in teaching people to write reports, letters or memos, make video programmes or produce brochures. The New Vocationalism takes up elements in 'progressivism' and stresses student-centred activity—and yet this emphasis on 'doing things' can lead to a lack of the necessary *reflection* on action and the detailed analysis which might provide students with rational social explanations for the predicament they find themselves in.

However, the stress on oral work, role-playing, group-work and 'realistic' situations need not be used in narrowly instrumental ways, but can raise discussions about problems at work or in the communitu around decision-making, collective action and responsibility. Issues around gender and race might be involved. For example, beginning with students' own experience in a part-time job or on work experience, an assignment could be based on a survey of the positions, salaries, promotion prospects, conditions of work of women and men in their workplace. The results of this survey could open up the whole area of equal opportunities, sexual discrimination, sexual harassment, rights at work and so on. This might not only help to equip the students for a possible job at the end of the course which they would enter with a greater awareness of the potential problems in this area, but also enable them to have a more 'global' view of women's/men's positions in society. This type of assignment could also be valuable when related to racial discrimination and the monitoring of equal opportunities amongst minority groups at work.

In ways like this, it may be possible to encourage what the authors of *Rewriting English* have called 'powerful literacy'—'the acquisition of those relevant forms of writing and reading and speaking that confer genuine understanding and control'[5], or what Raymond Williams advocated, back in 1961:

> Extensive practice in democratic procedures, including meetings, negotiations and the selection and conduct of leaders in democratic organisations. Extensive practice in the use of libraries, newspapers and magazines, radio and television programmes, and other resources of information, opinion and influence.[6]

Student assignments around recommendations for improving, say, leisure facilities in the area, or taking collective action about local planning, or collectively organizing events or research or presentations, can help to promote these aims.

Of course, young people do need to learn the skills necessary in getting what jobs there are and keeping them (and perhaps improving them). Yet such courses might also seek to educate young people in several directions: not only to provide them with atomized 'skills', but also a form of 'communications' which encourages them to be analytical, critical and creative as well. We believe that role-play, simulations, video-making, appropriate case studies, debates about social issues and even creative writing can all have a part to play in the New Vocationalism.[7]

We have so far tried to suggest ways in which formal structures of 'English' are changing in Further Education, and how teachers can attempt to work within them. These methods are more and more trying to take into account students' pre-existing and changing cultures and to promote student activity.

We as teachers do feel the need to take into account student cultures, to get to know and respond to particular students and cultural formations in a classroom. Now, of course, this *can* be a more efficient way of controlling 'them' (keeping 'them' quiet and interested); it *can* lead to greater surveillance (more detailed, more personal student records); it *can* lead to more thorough selection: but like all theories-from-above, there is a from-below version too: it can change *you*, it can alter the way you think about your subject, what you want to teach, how and why.

In this connection it is interesting to speculate on some of the origins of 'Cultural Studies'. Arguably, in the late fifties and early sixties Cultural Studies emerged out of a twilight, marginal world of evening classes, WEA, Trade Union classes, extra-mural departments, rather than mainstream university sites (note the early careers of figures central to Cultural Studies: E. P. Thompson, Raymond Williams, Richard Hoggart and, later, Stuart Hall). Teaching adults (waged, unwaged and in the home) is different, challenging in other ways, from teaching straight-from-school full-time students in a college or university. Received traditions of English or History may not be adequate. The 'outside world' may barge its way challengingly into the classroom more, particularly if the teacher is interested to learn from the students, as well as the other way round . . .

Another connection can be made in this context: with 'progressive' English teaching, or some strands within it. English teachers in schools have often asked students to talk and write from 'experience': autobiographies, people they know, neighbourhoods, childhood, activities, descriptions, part-time jobs . . . This is often linked with a pedagogy which values the 'personal', expressive informal talk, 'coming to know . . .', talk and writing which are—to begin with—tentative and exploratory.[8] Such teaching sometimes opens up channels of communication by the use of log-books or journals for students' informal comments, jokes, memories, questions. Another way is to use detailed questionnaires as a starting point: what do students read/watch/listen to/do outside the institution/ want to do in the future/get angry about? (We find this provides a common frame of reference for subsequent discussions and opens up negotiations for an agenda for future study.)

In the debates about 'the Crisis in English', or even within Cultural Studies, students' positions and perspectives often get left out. If we don't believe any more that media 'audiences' are *passive*, and we think that readers *transform* texts, then so too learners have to be seen as *agents*—as well as, no doubt, victims. (Of course, the actual ways in which students react to classes will be many, varied, layered and—in the end—probably unknowable by teachers.)

Although these points suggest the importance of progressivist methods, there are problems with taking up progressivism in any simple way. Such methods do encourage the bringing in of (some of) students' cultural experience into the classroom, yet they also might legitimate a version of experience which is highly individualistic, unique, 'natural' and fixed. This does not go easily with 'Cultural Studies' theories which suggest (however tentatively) the wider social maps which structure our consciousness and culture collectively: theories of class and of women's oppression, histories of imperialism and racism, materialist and structuralist theories of language, not to mention theories of the repressed and unconscious. These 'social maps' seem necessarily abstract and therefore difficult to teach by progressive methods. At best, progressivism seems to suggest that learning moves outwards from the personal and the concrete to the global and the abstract in ever-increasing concentric circles. Yet the movement outwards from say, the breakfast table in front of you to the workings of multinational industries in the Third World is something that involves dizzying jumps.[9] This tension, between what is immediate, local and 'experiential' to the learner and what is far-off and 'abstract' (yet determining), is a central factor in most teaching, and perhaps it is important that teaching has to be about bridge-building between the two.

'Experience' is a difficult category anyway, of course.[10] When someone talks or writes from 'experience' all kinds of values, judgements, omissions are present, as if naturalized. In the same way as the Oral History movement (with its wonderful slogan, 'Dig Where You Stand!') can sometimes be criticized for naturalizing experience, so too can the English-from-Experience school. However, we find that, in conditions of some trust, talking and writing from experience are a way of beginning a discussion which can then move towards wider social determinants: how representative is it, or how individual? why did it happen like that? suppose you had been a woman/man? suppose you had been black/white? how does the way you talk or write affect what you've said? and so on.[11]

For example, in a 'Media and Cultural Studies' class, a student of ours has just written about the pleasures and rituals of being a 'Mod'. He knows far more about the details and the 'experience' than we do (or than most of the published accounts). Yet we can begin to ask questions which put that experience into a wider context (about social aspirations, the views of parents, gender-relations and so on). In such a collaborative process, we would hope to learn something too, and have our 'academic' preconceptions deepened and challenged . . .

Sometimes cultural formations in classrooms are very obviously not simply individual, of course. Cultural groupings and divisions within classrooms—like distinct ethnic or gender cultural differences—require a response from teachers and syllabuses. For instance, in multi-cultural colleges many students' needs are seldom met by the rigid confines of traditional monocultural 'English' or vocational syllabuses. Even so, in multi-ethnic colleges, lecturers sometimes assume, for example, that they are always 'fair' because, to quote a comment frequently met with, 'I treat them all the same'. However, this dismissal of students' different backgrounds can become a form of covert racism: students' relationships to the same monocultural material will differ, advantaging some, disadvantaging others. It has to be demonstrated that groups' diverse cultures are both valuable and valued by teachers, by syllabuses and by other students. Sadly, too often you can read Asian students' essays in which the central characters are white rather than Asian and in which the settings and situations have nothing to do with the real life of the students writing about them. The arguments about a multicultural anti-racist teaching need to be translated into a practice . . . [12]

Similarly gender issues cannot be ignored in the classroom. For one thing, gender-culture divisions within the same classroom can be extreme. In a YTS group that one of us has taught there are eight young men and seven young women. The classroom has a central aisle, and unless they are moved, the men sit on the one side, and the women on the other. (This description will be necessarily superficial, and it's going to sound like caricature, but this is how it seems externally.) The young women are neat. 'feminine', dressed in fashionable pastels and baggy slacks, their appearance immaculate. In free moments they huddle together and talk quietly, swapping photographs, talking about work and people they know. The young men include a group of five friends, near-classic 'lads', who put down the other three with sexual and physical insults. The lads are loud and take up lots of space. Some of them are very big physically, and the impression is that they are scruffy incredible hulks . . . The lads imitate other teachers behind their backs, insult each other, brag about how many pints they're going to have down the pub at dinner time. When asked, the women think the lads are 'immature' and 'stupid'—the men that they are interested in must be better than this: older and with higher job status. If the lads cross the women a strong put-down (often sexual) wings across the classroom from the women. However, in group work, to mix the women with the men may well be physically intimidating for the women. (When suggestions about mixing are made, it is the women who challenge it.[13])

Not all mixed YTS groups are like this, but it focuses tendencies in an extreme form. Any well-worked-out long-term teacher response would have to take into account the ways in which these different gender/class-cultures are strategies both for survival and towards certain goals.[14] However, in the short term, teachers have to find ways of coping—for instance, in this case, ways of not letting the lads dominate discussion. Something that did seem to work with this group was in role-play to cast the women in authoritative positions as chairperson or speakers ...

In less polarized groups different methods might work. Although there is still probably a place for the much-debated 'A woman's place is in the home' (yawn), perhaps (as we've theorized above) one of the most successful ways to raise levels of awareness and begin a discussion around gender is to use the group's own experiences as a starting point.

However, getting down to talking about gender issues is not always straightforward (particularly for a woman teacher). A familiar reaction from the boys (and sometimes the girls) is 'Oh no, s/he's not on about feminism again!', which immediately causes antagonism and forces the atmosphere to deteriorate before the session has even begun.

One relatively successful way to combat this is to set the group a familiar-sounding task and to separate them into single sex groups to work on it. (This is done for at least two reasons: to allow greater freedom of expression, and to combat feelings of overt hostility between the sexes, which there are sometimes.)

An example of this in action was when one 'O' Level English group (five young men and ten young women) were separated into two groups to investigate 'what girls/boys talk about'. They were equipped with flip charts and felt tips to record their ideas. They were asked to begin by recollecting a recent conversation they had experienced with members of the same sex and to produce a list of topics that they talked about. They were also asked to compile a list of subjects that they considered were most talked about by the opposite sex. And they had to attempt to answer the broader question, 'Are the subjects that boys and girls talk about different? If so, why?' They would later get together in one large group to exchange their ideas.

The structured and segregated beginning proved to be successful, not only as a tactical method of breaking into the subject (a lengthy and fruitful discussion ensued), but it also held valuable lessons for those taking part. For example, at one point the boys' group felt that they had completed the work and therefore requested a break. They mingled with other students in the canteen and discussed the ideas they had arrived at, seeking approval in one instance from a female student who was appalled at their suggestions. (They had included on their list 'picking up birds', drinking, sex and football.) They became acutely aware of the limited and stereotyped vision they had imposed on their sex through the list they had compiled and, as a direct consequence of this encounter, they altered the list quite dramatically for the plenary session with the women. They seemed to undergo a definite change of mood—it was as if they realized that the 'laddish'/'macho' image they had presented was unacceptable and they now wished to be taken seriously. More acceptable 'adult' topics of conversation (though equally 'masculine') like 'politics', replaced the violently scored out 'Samantha Fox'.

Another valuable lesson that emerged from the session was the visible growth in confidence among the women. Not only did they work closely as a group, carefully discussing and sharing ideas, but they also demanded that they should be in total control of the discussion, without feeling inhibited by the presence of a teacher who might intervene at any moment!

This did help to raise students' consciousness about gender issues, and we do feel that the area of talk is an important one. On formal occasions (for example, in 'oral' examinations) we have become acutely aware that the young men *tend* to talk impersonally and 'objectively' with encyclopedic knowledge of computers, sports, sailing, skiing, musical instruments, facts, things, facts, things. Young women *tend* to talk expressively about families, holidays, part-time jobs—often perceptively and with humour. Yet the boys' mode is a high-status public knowledge form that will help them 'get on', even though perhaps emotionally limiting them...

So we are suggesting that teachers have to try to be aware of unequal power relations within a class and to attempt to make careful interventions. Another strategy we have tried sometimes (one which raises useful arguments) is to suggest that in group work we would prefer the person who takes the notes to be male and the person who reports back to be female. But—as always—it depends on the group.

A central move in 'progressive education' is usually towards student participation of all kinds, in an apparent transfer of power, initiative and choice away from the teacher and towards students. We now want to instance three examples of this, and to suggest some problems.

The first example is of English 'A' Level students organizing a dayschool for students on the same course at other schools and colleges. As this took place during a period when NATFHE[15] was working to rule, teacher involvement in preparations had to be minimal. The student group constituted itself as a working party and delegated responsibilities: negotiating with college management, publicity, letters, hiring videos and selecting stimulus material. More importantly they had to decide on whether they wanted small-group work and how best to set this up (in the end they settled for pairs of friends with another pair from another centre), the best way to introduce each other, the right kind of questions to ask about chosen topics. They decided (probably rightly) to exclude teachers from the group discussions on the day . . . and we as teachers became almost extraneous to the learning process, just another resource.

In ways like this, groups can begin to teach themselves. Yet, of course, some of their material, ideas and methods drew off things we had set up earlier in the course and elsewhere. This activity would not have been possible early in their time with us at college. It is very difficult for teachers to let go (or loose) the reins and trust the student group—sometimes with just cause. However, this seemed to work: there was a good deal of collaborative learning and activity which it was exciting to watch.

Another example of students assuming some control over their learning activity was when, again on a first-year 'A' Level English course, it was suggested that as a way of appreciating information found in Beatrix Campbell's *Wigan Pier Revisited* the group should spend some of their time collecting information on their town's unemployed—as a method of assessing the difficulties of selecting material, interviewing, and as a means of comparing unemployment in the industrial wastelands of the North and Coventry with the more rural but now also deindustrialized town where the college is.

The group organized itself and planned the project, which meant many hours of group discussion. Questionnaires were devised, strategies for interviews worked out and eventually the project would be written up and typed. They ventured out of the classroom and into the town where they interviewed families in their homes, people on council estates, the unemployed outside the dole office and inside the Job Centre, and staff and bureaucrats in the local council offices.

Although most of them knew of young people who were facing the prospect of long-term unemployment, many of the group had no knowledge of how widespread unemployment was in the area or how unemployment would affect lifestyles or morale. The project not only helped them to appreciate these factors, it also opened up their eyes to housing problems in the area and made them more confident about approaching the public. However, the most positive and noticeable aspect of the project was the confidence it gave the group—particularly in relation to making collective decisions and organizing themselves.

There are problems with handing over to students too. With an Art Foundation 'Media and Cultural Studies' course which two of us had been teaching, realizing that in the past we'd talked too much, we suggested that members of the group 'take' parts of lessons or whole lessons. Therefore, when members (four out of twenty) approached us, asking if they could take a class which had been billed on our 'flexible' 'negotiable' syllabus as 'The Meaning of Pop Music', we accepted—with the proviso that we would help plan the lesson.

Yet we were also very busy. Planning time was mostly spent duplicating material the students wanted to use. In the end we had to place our confidence in the students. We heard some of their points, made sure they had a running order, looked at some questions—but that was all.

As it turned out, one person (Mick) did most of the presentation. He made some strong points, and some others. One was that although an audience might interpret a song in one way, if you read the lyrics carefully the 'real' purpose can be the opposite of this. Mick tended to interpret this as 'this is what it means, and if they don't see it like this they're stupid'. And Mick's nervousness resulted in what looked like over-confidence and a dismissal of other people's points ('Yeah, well let's look at another lyric'). In the discussion at the end, we (feeling the need to be *liberal* and open up space for other points of view) asked if some people had other views or interpretations. Various points that *we* thought important were lost: that the music, singers and this style of presentation were extremely *macho*; that it may matter more what *most people* make of songs rather than the minority who scrutinize lyrics; that the overall 'image' of the group (clothes, styles, marketing) may matter more than what lyrics mean; and much more.

So, what was learned from this experience? Well, the four presenters had done work as a group, organizing and arranging, planning co-operatively—even if one dominated in the presentation itself. Secondly, they did learn skills as presenters—and some of the presentation was impressive and well thought-through. Thirdly, perhaps, everyone saw that students can be 'teachers' and 'experts' too. (This was an area of 'relevance' to their own interests: it might not have been possible to engage that degree of participation on another subject.)

And what can we learn about 'progressive' methods from this? Perhaps that group work needs to be developed little by little: skills of sensitivity to others' points and making space for others are essential; perhaps that it is important to move out of the immediately relevant towards more general, more questioning concepts; perhaps that the whole group needs to move *together*.

So, the transfer of power is difficult. Alarm bells sometimes go off in teachers' heads about not enough participation from all members, about offensiveness to some people in the group, about not enough concepts, and more. We would hope that our students could learn to be sensitive to these problems too.

In this article we have suggested how 'English' is changing within Further Education, and how teachers might try to relate to students' cultural formations and differing demands. However, as we claimed earlier, students are not merely passive and what 'effects' a lesson may have are often difficult to predict or know. For one thing, in any form of institutional education—including 'progressive' versions—there will be resistance and reserve, probably rightly. For example, we rather admire the cool and the distance of the 'quiet' student (even if we don't agree with her!) who wrote in her notebook after a class:

> I felt the lesson had been well structured and made as interesting as possible and the lecturers had obviously spent a lot of time preparing it. However, I did feel it was organized in such a way that one couldn't help siding with the feminists and therefore it was perhaps a little biased.

Or—more positively—students may follow up for themselves something that has interested them in the classroom. Such was the impact of studying one black poet on three students (two black and one Asian) that they attended their first Arts Festival where the poet was appearing. Afterwards all three students approached the poet and one of them thanked the writer for doing so much for black people and said how much the poetry had meant to him personally. 'Don't thank me,' the writer responded. 'If you feel so strongly about it, write poetry yourself.' This was a watershed for the student, who did try writing and found he could do so with much excitement.

Notes

[1] The Youth Training Scheme: now two years for those of sixteen and over; it involves a 'placement' at a workplace and, usually, some 'off-the-job' training in an educational establishment; trainees are given an 'allowance'.
The Certificate of Pre-Vocational Education: a school or college course for sixteen-year-olds, offering them 'tasters' of types of vocational training.
The Technical and Vocational Education Initiative: vocational courses for fourteen-year-olds and over.

[2] The National Association of Teachers of English (NATE) publishes a useful survey of such syllabuses: *Alternatives at English A-Level*, NATE Examinations Booklet number 4 (Exeter 1982)—soon to be updated.
Accounts of rewards and problems of such 'alternative' syllabuses can be found in Roy Goddard, 'Beyond the Literary Heritage: Meeting the Needs of English at 16–19', *English in Education*, Vol. 19, no. 2 (Summer 1985), pp. 12–22, and the contributions by Jim Porteous and Stephen Bennison, and Cathy Bowden in *Literature Teaching Politics 6 1985: Conference Papers*, compiled and edited by Helen Taylor (Bristol, 1985).

[3] Alan Bleasdale, *Boys from the Blackstuff* (St. Albans, 1982); Buchi Emecheta, *Second-Class Citizen* (Glasgow, 1977); Amrit Wilson, *Finding A*

Voice (London, 1978); Beatrix Campbell, *Wigan Pier Revisited* (London, 1984); eds John Brown and David Jackson, *Varieties of Writing* (Basingstoke, 1984).

[4] Youth Opportunities Programme, later replaced by the Youth Training Scheme; Work Experience on Employers' Premises; Training Opportunities Programme.

[5] Janet Batsleer, Tony Davies, Rebecca O'Rourke and Chris Weedon, *Rewriting English* (London, 1985), p. 165.

[6] Raymond Williams, *The Long Revolution* (Harmondsworth, 1973 edition), p. 175.

[7] For a detailed critique of the philosophy of the New Vocationalism and a positive alternative, see Janet Batsleer, 'Life Skills and Social Education', *Youth and Policy*, no. 15, Winter 1985–6, pp. 9–14. See also Philip Cohen, 'Against the New Vocationalism' in Inge Bates et al., *Schooling for the Dole?* (Basingstoke, 1984), pp. 104–69.

[8] One detailed (and adventurous) account of this kind of teaching is Peter Medway's *Finding A Language: Autonomy and Learning in School* (London, 1980).

[9] Yet see the opening of Nigel Harris, *Of Bread and Guns* (Harmondsworth, 1983). These progressivist difficulties are examined by Medway in *Finding A Language*, pp. 71–2.

[10] For some succinct discussion of 'experience', see E. P. Thompson, 'The Politics of Theory' in *People's History and Socialist Theory*, ed. Raphael Samuel (London, 1981), esp. pp. 406–7, and Perry Anderson, *Arguments Within English Marxism* (London, 1980), pp. 25–30.

[11] For related and parallel issues, see CCCS Popular Memory Group, 'Popular Memory: theory, politics, method' in Centre for Contemporary Cultural Studies, *Making Histories* (London, 1982), pp. 205–52.

[12] Difficult issues that we can only touch on here are discussed more fully in the ILEA English Centre's *The English Curriculum: Race* (London, n.d.), for example.

[13] This might sound like an argument for single-sex classes. However, for every all-women class, there usually has to be an all-men class, and this enhances not only the confidence of the women but also the male culture. For discussion of these issues, see Pat Mahony, *Schools for the Boys?* (London, 1985).

[14] See the work of Paul Willis on 'lads' and their culture in Paul Willis, *Learning to Labour* (London, 1977). On young women, see: Angela McRobbie, 'Working Class Girls and the culture of femininity' in Women's Studies Group CCCS, *Women Take Issue* (London, 1978); Christine Griffin, *Typical Girls? Young Women from School to the Job Market* (London, 1985); Angela McRobbie and Mica Nava, eds, *Gender and Generation* (Basingstoke, 1984). We hope that related work by Joyce Canaan and Robert Hollands, ethno-

graphic researchers at the Centre for Contemporary Cultural Studies will soon be published. We as teachers might learn much from such youth and classroom 'ethnographies'.

[15] National Association of Teachers in Further and Higher Education.

Damning the Tides: The New English and The Reviewers

TONY DAVIES

'What does it mean, to "read English"?' The question might be thought both rhetorical and disingenuous, but when I asked it, in 1982, in an essay in Peter Widdowson's *Re-Reading English*, I didn't, I think, intend it to be either.[1] Simply, it seemed to me that in the already energetically proliferating debate about the role of 'theory' and the history and ideological import of the discipline, too little thought had been given to the relationship—at one level a deepening estrangement, all too easily exploited by enemies of the newer work, at another, a difficult and uneven kind of 'popularization'—between elaborated theory and the seemingly quite untheoretical day-to-day teaching of the subject.

None of the contributors to *Re-Reading English*, that so unexpectedly celebrated venture, had any premonition of just how deep and persistent the trauma occasioned by its appearance would prove, nor how luridly revealing its symptoms. But throughout the whole windy and opinionated affair, one voice was notably absent from the acrimonious polyphony of the correspondence columns in the trade papers: the voice of those thousands of students who actually do—in the practical, subordinate position—'read' as well as—critically, theoretically, disenchantedly—'re-read' English. Not that the students themselves were entirely absent from the debate. On the contrary, they provided one of its signal points of reference, as objects of protective solicitude, professorial condescension and plangent mid-life disenchantment. But it is precisely as *objects* that they featured throughout, placed intransitively at the opposite pole to the scholarly professionalism of their teachers. The whole episode was profoundly revealing of *that*, suggesting a different question, one even more neglected than the first: not 'what does it mean to read English?', but what, in these days, does it mean to *teach* it?

Re-Reading English came out in March 1982. But John Bayley had already set the tone—or one tone, a languid Oxonian *hauteur*—earlier in the year in a *TLS* review of Jonathan Culler's *Pursuit of Signs*.[2] Although structuralism, he opined, may have brainwashed the first-year students of some university literature courses into using jargon as a mode of response, its influence on the upper echelons has been on the whole invigorating. Such fashions are for the elite; can they ever be effectively popularized, instead of just ideologically imposed?

Key terms circulate here, in a series of recurrent tropes. 'Theory' is fundamentally trivial, a succession of modish or eccentric poses impelled by an internal logic of novelty and sensationalism ('as fashion pursues its way, the seductive or daunting façade of semiotics begins to fragment . . .'). And like the fashion business, the academic world consists of an elite of intellectual *couturiers* moving in tiny, narcissistic circles, and a mass-market of cheap and vulgarized imitations. 'Popularization' is an important and complex issue, and Bayley touches on real problems when he contrasts it with 'imposition'; but even as he touches them, his complacent ironies devalue all the central questions and prepare the way for a defensive retreat into bluff common sense (in a later *TLS* piece, he was to dismiss the 'crisis in English' as bogus, contrasting the 'minority of activists' with that 'silent majority of students' stolidly indifferent to their agitations).[3]

But as Bayley's metaphors indicate, theory-as-couture lapses continually, with a more ominous cadence, into theory-as-indoctrination ('brainwashed', 'ideologically imposed'); and if in the first formulation students appear as rude mechanicals, uncomprehendingly aping the intellectual manners of their betters ('using jargon as a mode of response'), in the second they figure, with a more urgent stress, as victims of an academic thermidor. 'They appear', said one reviewer of the contributors to *Re-Reading English*, 'to be members of a dissident intelligentsia which is preparing the theoretical ground from which an English National Liberation Army may one day emerge'.[4] Culler's book, with its studied reasonableness and coolly agnostic pluralism, makes a poor target for a polemic in this key, and Bayley had to be content, for his more minatory flourishes, with vague, anonymous adversaries like 'structuralism' and 'semiotics'. But there was thunder in the air in the spring of 1982. The McCabe affair in Cambridge still rumbled ominously, and a Penguin special by McCabe and Stephen Heath was promised later in the year (it never came). The first round of Joseph/UGC cuts, announced the previous summer, had energized and radicalized, as their successors were to demoralize; and on all sides there was a sense of issues polarized and positions sharply seen, a tense anticipation of conflict. The 1981 Literature Teaching Politics conference had been held, appropriately enough, in Cambridge, and the excitement, as a decade of theoretical reflection seemed about to swing into the active mode, had been palpable. By 1982, in Birmingham, where the opening plenary was interrupted by news of the launching of the Falklands task force, the stresses and complexities of reading, teaching, *being* 'English' seemed close to breaking-point, and the crisis which—it was reported on all sides—the subject was undergoing looked suddenly like the local manifestation of some much deeper disorder, a historic *dénouement* in the culture of Englishness.

In this charged and bristling atmosphere, *Re-Reading English* worked like a lightning-conductor. Of course the metaphor is misleading: actually there was nothing very natural or spontaneous about the critical reception which was organized for the book. 'Organized' is the right word, not because the uniformly hostile, indeed abusive reviews the book received in this country resulted from editorial collusion (though such things are not unheard-of), but because everything about its reception—the choice of reviewers, the timing and context of the reviews, the decision to treat the book, and the series in which it appeared, as a symptomatic case, the rhetorical strategies employed to ridicule and denounce it— all pointed to an unusual convergence of values, means and purposes of the kind that give plausibility to the notion of a literary 'establishment'.

Not all the reviews fell into this pattern. Some were straightforwardly and independently hostile, from the standpoint of a traditional academic conservatism. Arthur Pollard, in one of the first reviews, trundled out the creaking old *canard* about the 'Marxist infiltration of literary studies', sneered at Polytechnics, and summoned to his side the gaunt spectre of those 'absolute moral and spiritual values that Leavis saw as fundamental'.[5] For Pollard, at least, nothing has changed. All talk of a 'crisis in English studies' is 'self-created fantasy', and the enemy, as ever, is an undifferentiated and unchanging 'Marxism' whose 'subversive intent' can be traced to 'such organizations as the Birmingham Centre for Cultural Studies (*sic*), the Open University and the CNAA'. It may seem surprising that stuff like this can get into print nowadays, even in the not especially discriminating pages of *British Book News*. But Pollard's tone—xenophobic, anti-intellectual and stridently abusive— resonated perfectly with the orchestrated jingoism and violent rhetoric of the Falklands–Malvinas episode: a dispiritingly typical illustration of the renewed confidence and bravado of academic reaction in that grim period. But although those accents were to recur in later reviews, the saloon-bar banality of Pollard's world view, like the vacuous pomposity of his 'absolute moral and spiritual values', belongs to an earlier period—the period, perhaps, of the Macarthyite *Gould Report*—and is not characteristic of the book's reception as a whole.

The keynote reviews of *Re-Reading English*, and the correspondence they provoked, appeared in three periodicals, each of them strategically positioned in its own part of the literary-political terrain: the *Times Literary Supplement* (weekly, editor Jeremy Treglown), the *London Review of Books* (roughly fortnightly, editor Karl Miller) and *PNReview* (two-monthly, editor Michael Schmidt). These three don't of course share anything like a common editorial programme. Indeed, they don't, with the possible exception of *PNR*, display an explicit inclination of any kind. Still less is there reason to suppose that their reviewing policies are the result of some kind of conspiratorial *mise-en-scène*. Nonetheless, regular readers will have no difficulty in identifying a distinctive political flavour common to all three, a set of generically-related attitudes and responses ranging from Sissonian neo-traditionalism (*PNR*) through acerbic fogeyishness (*LRB*) to an upholstered and patrician conservatism by turns unctuous and fastidiously dismissive. Editorial 'presence' varies accordingly. *PNR* editorializes energetically— especially its 'contributing editor' Nicolas Tredell, who is forever manufacturing pseudo-debates, quasi-controversies and *ersatz* colloquia on half-baked or non-existent issues. At *LRB* the editor confines his speaking-role largely to an acidulous obligato on the letters page, snapping at his correspondents' heels like a dyspeptic poodle ('Mr—'s first sentence is exquisitely typical of one kind of polemical writer on this subject' ... 'It would seem that Mr—can hardly fail to do well at Cambridge' etc.). Treglown at the *TLS* observes, in his own pages at least, the traditional anonymity of that curious and influential paper, a Prospero-like aloofness and invisibility bizarrely at odds with the chosen style of his proprietor and his Wapping colleagues. Together, they constitute a potent trinity— three independent fingers still capable of converging, when needed, into a fist.

LRB was first in the field—but only, it seems, as a result of a curious incident. Two members of the English Department at Nottingham University were invited to review the book. *TLS* sent it to Roger Poole, a senior member of the department and a seasoned reviewer whose broad literary interests and familiarity with recent theory promised an interesting and informed critique. *LRB* called up his younger and much less experienced colleague Tom Paulin, whose qualifications for the job are harder to locate. Paulin's review—a weirdly unbalanced, at times almost demented effort— duly appeared. Poole's did not, and throughout the autumn rumour whispered that Treglown had declined to publish his piece, purportedly on grounds of 'style', and had commissioned another, from a different reviewer. Eventually, in December, *TLS* did carry a review of the book, by Claude Rawson from the University of Warwick[6]—a review marked throughout by signs of haste, inconsistency and a curious underlying ambivalence, surely one of the least distinguished, and worst written, pieces this reputable eighteenth-century scholar has ever committed to print.

Meanwhile, copies of Poole's typescript were circulating widely, and replying to Paulin's review, Peter Widdowson alluded to the incident in a letter to *LRB*: 'the *TLS* has, I gather, finally found it an unequivocally hostile reviewer so that it will be well and truly smashed there'.[7] This evoked no response. But some time later Antony Easthope, another *RRE* contributor, repeated the charge more circumstantially in a letter to *PNR*. Describing Rawson's review as a 'hysterical denunciation', he continued:

> However, this *TLS* review was actually the *second* review of the book commissioned by Rupert Murdoch's newspaper. The first praised the New Accents series as 'a most intelligent and coherent contribution to literary studies' and said that *Re-Reading English* was a book 'everyone should read'. This review was turned down. Possibly it was rejected on stylistic grounds; but it is very unusual for the *TLS* to commission a second review rather than ask for the first to be revised.[8]

This time Treglown replied, confirming that he had turned down the first review, 'not . . . because it favoured the new criticism, but because in my view and the Deputy Editor's it was irredeemably weakly argued and badly written'.[9] And now at last Roger Poole, the hitherto anonymous subject of so much speculation and contumely, emerged, blinking in the unaccustomed glare, to offer his own account:

> When I sent my review in, it was turned down 'on stylistic grounds'. I was told on the phone that the piece was so badly written that, not only was it unprintable, but it was also *unrevisable*.... When I finally read (Rawson's) review ... I wrote to the Editor of the *TLS*, to point out that 'the whole review as published is an interesting proof that, if a reviewer's ideological prejudices fit in with received opinion at the *TLS*, then the editor and sub-editor will actually pass and allow to be printed far worse 'style' than anything an independently-minded reviewer will be allowed' ... he rang to tell me that I was quite wrong about Rawson's style, that it was really very good, and that I should go away and read the review again.[10]

The third member of the *troika*, *PNR*, had already carried a review by Nicolas Tredell earlier in the year:[11] more temperate than the others, but veering like them towards panic and falling back, on the central issue of evaluation (the book's arguments on which were crudely travestied by Paulin as the belief 'that sonnets and beer mats ought to be treated on an equal footing'), on a tired empiricism: 'Most students will know already, not from bourgeois ideology, but through their experience of reading, that they prefer some authors to others'. But it was soon apparent that Tredell envisaged a campaign, indeed a crusade, against 'the New Accents crowd' (Treglown) on a front far wider than could be provided by a review of a single specimen, albeit one so conveniently many-headed and irresistibly provocative. *PNR* 37 featured an editorial sermon on the 'The Politicization of English' in which once again New Accents figured largely ('Hawkes, Belsey and Bennett are now well-established on students' reading-lists ...'); and in *PNR* 48 Tredell and Schmidt offered an even more portentous piece of self-advertising pomposity, a Wittenberg declaration of seven theses entitled 'A New Orthodoxy' ('the problem is less one of Marxism *per se* than of its fusion with other elements of orthodoxy ...'), which enjoined us 'to continue to discriminate, with vigour, among literary texts ... to ensure that traditional critical approaches remain active and available', and so on—to subscribe, as though to some shockingly controversial new notion, to the *old* orthodoxy.

This implausible attempt to reconvene an ancient Leavisite light infantry for a last great Agincourt against the common enemy seems to have flopped. Of those invited to subscribe most were either puzzled, indifferent or openly contemptuous. A similar reception has so far attended other attempts to reconstitute, or reinvent, a 'traditional' literary-critical consensus. *Critical Quarterly* retains a combative edge, but thanks largely to regular contributions (Sinfield, Eagleton) from the other side of the wire. Laurence Lerner's *Reconstructing Literature* had been generally conceded, even by its chums, to be eccentric, aimless and feeble. The late Helen Gardner's *In Defence of the Imagination*, though prescribed by Arthur Pollard as the 'proper antidote' to the virulent toxins of New Accents 'Marxism', is actually disappointingly thin, querulous and uncertain of its target. This is genuinely a pity. Intellectual culture thrives on vigorous and informed debate, and good criticism and theory of literature (inevitably, as Tredell recognised, 'also a debate about culture, education, politics, society')[12] has always generated a strong undertow of polemic and critique. The real indicator of a 'crisis' in English literary culture is not the appearance of adversarial counter-criticisms and combatively deconstructive theory (never, in any case, remotely approaching the scale or coherence of a new 'orthodoxy') but the exhaustion of a set of traditional discourses (Arnoldian, New-Critical, Leavisite) which nevertheless continue to comprise, albeit in a curiously abstract and enervated form, the dominant repertoire and conceptual substructure of most university English departments, where, increasingly, they require conformity while less and less commanding assent.

How is this possible? Well, one explanation, as I suggested in that *Re-Reading English* piece, may be that while the journals, the research and publication, the conferences and staff seminars and other kinship rituals of Eng. Lit. academics are preoccupied with the entrepreneurial cultural capital of criticism and theory, their departments, and above all the students in them, are inescapably caught up in the experiential primacy and raw materiality of *teaching*. The gulf separating the two activities has undoubtedly been widened in recent years by the fact that teaching has virtually no status in the assessment of academic competence. It occupies a position in the academic economy not unlike that of domestic labour in the wider society, at once unvalued and indispensable. But teaching has also proved, in higher education in Britain, staunchly resistant to the influence of the speculative and theoretical temper, not so much because English teachers in higher education are uniformly un- or anti-theoretical (though some of the most influential teacher-critics have been, aggressively, both) but because of the formal and historical character of the activity itself.

It would be useful and instructive to have a proper history of teaching: not of education (there are more than enough of those) but of the institutional and the lived relations, the ideological-discursive economy of pedagogy. It would be a vast enterprise, in a society for which education has often served as a point of convergence for a whole complex of social fears and motivations. But a suggestive starting-point, for the modern period, might be provided by Milton's definition of the ideal schoolmaster:

> But here (the academic curriculum) the main skill and groundwork will be, to temper them such lectures and explanations upon every opportunity, as may lead and draw them in willing obedience, inflamed with the study of learning, and the admiration of virtue; stirred up with high hopes of living to be brave men, and worthy patriots, dear to God, and famous to all ages . . . which he who hath the Art, and proper eloquence to catch them with, what with mild and effectual persuasions, and what with the intimation of some fear, if need be, but chiefly by his own example, might in a short space gain them to an incredible diligence and courage.[13]

For the humanist educators of the sixteenth and seventeenth centuries, the important changes lay not so much in the shift from a theological to a classical curriculum, or the adoption of Hellenic and Roman ideals of individual development and civic responsibility, as in a novel conception of the role of the teacher and the character of an effective pedagogy, a conception suggested by Milton's definition of the intimate, familial and exemplary character of the teaching relationship and encapsulated in the phrase 'willing obedience', the ideal congruence of the teacher's authority and the co-operation of the pupil, persuasion and fear. Large historical themes come into view at this point; for the evolution of modern European nation states, in all the variety of their social and institutional formations, has indeed been the story of the pursuit by social forces struggling into maturity and taking possession of the means of self-representation of just such a 'hegemonic' fusion of coercion and consent, the 'willing obedience' of the conquered, the colonized and the subordinated. Milton, shortly to become a functionary and ideologue of the Cromwellian commonwealth, elaborates his educational and social programme from the centre of these developments; and although the claims of force and persuasion are urged across a wide spectrum of public and private discourses (in arguments about marriage and divorce, about religious liberty and conformity, about political representation and the rights of the people), the central and organizing instance and point of reference remains, in the mid-seventeenth century, the 'advancement of learning': a reformed national education, grounded in a new pedagogy.

In England, as the case of Milton illustrates, these humanist themes are given a puritan inflection. Models of schooling are drawn not only from the ideal academies of the ancients and the Tudor educationalists but from the structure and ethos of the dissenting congregation. There, in strong contrast to the Roman and high Anglican hierarchies, truth and salvation are sought not in the unquestionable authority of the church but in the promptings—supported to be sure by the egalitarian neighbourliness of the conventicle—of individual conscience, guided spiritually by the benevolent seniority of a pastor or 'lecturer' whose status in turn derives not from any external, coercive authority but from the free consent and 'willing obedience' of the congregation itself.

After the Restoration, those noncomforming puritans unwilling to subscribe a token allegiance to the state church were excluded from many schools and from the universities of Oxford and Cambridge; and the alternative network of 'Dissenting Academies' that they founded inherited the transitive, consensual pedagogy of Milton's *Tractate*, with its quasi-familial conception of the teacher as guide and friend and its stress on the motivation rather than the compulsion to learn. And those academies provided, in turn, the institutional groundwork not only for the corresponding societies, mechanics' institutes and working men's colleges in which the new industrial classes and their radical intelligentsias found an education but also for the university colleges in London and the manufacturing towns; bequeathing to them, too, their curricular utilitarianism, their preference for a vernacular and modern over a classical and antiquarian syllabus, above all their conception of education not as the handing-down of certain given knowledges within a process of specified professional or academic training, but as the nurturing of integral social subjectivities, an activity, as in Milton, at once pervasively coercive, since the teacher has access to every corner of the student's life, and freely chosen.

The reality, of course, is rather different, not least because the Miltonic harmony of fear and persuasion is in actuality a contradiction, one which the latest heirs of the dissenting tradition, in comprehensive schools and redbrick universities and polytechnics and colleges, have had occasion in recent years to feel sharply. In arts and humanities, where the ethical mission of nonconformity with its notions of all-round character building and education for 'life' survives most strongly, and above all perhaps in English, which retains something of the secular evangelism with which it was charged by the Victorian pioneers of liberal education, teachers have frequently been expected to perform a repertoire of barely-compatible roles, shifting constantly from companionable intimacy and informality to surveillance, assessment, judgement—a repertoire that may account for the deep gratifications and compulsions of teaching, but that strikes many students, and some teachers, as a Pirandellian farrago of hypocrisy, equivocation and bad faith. At its worst it confuses teaching (and most university and polytechnic lecturers aren't even trained properly to do *that*) with 'counselling' and draws teachers and students into a kind of collusive lay psychiatry—a role which most are manifestly unsuited, and none actually qualified, to perform. But above all, teaching itself embodies the central ambivalence—the double sense of 'discipline'; one felt more strongly, on the whole, by younger and more 'radical' teachers and thus a focus, as the institution shifts into a defensive stance, both for student activism and for reactionary paranoia.

Which brings us back to *Re-Reading English*, and to the forlorn and frantically gesticulating figure of Tom Paulin. 'The crisis which now affects English studies', pontificated Paulin in his *LRB* review, 'is a reflection of a more general cultural atmosphere—for example, that futureless and pastless sense of blankness which is for various reasons the quality that distinguishes the present generation of students'. Never mind the passing thought that Tom Paulin's students may have their own good reasons, nearer home than the 'general cultural atmosphere', for looking blank; go into any university commonroom in Britain and you're pretty certain to hear someone holding forth on the subject of 'the present generation of students'. For some, like Paulin himself, the inevitable inferiority of the present generation to all previous ones and especially to the speaker's own betokens the decline of traditional literary scholarship and 'the sense of the past'. For others, the ones who like to remind you where they were in '68, it confirms the demise of the student activist and the onset of reactionary apathy. But the underlying syntax is constant, and the ascription of 'blankness', of a stranded vacancy both vulnerable and unresponsive, equivocates between the kindly concern of the solicitous tutor and the bored dismissiveness of the embittered 'don'.

'Students must be fairly warned against "New Accents".' Once or twice, the raw hostility evoked by the book emerged directly ('English . . . can only be rescued by . . . abolishing courses that draw on the kind of critical texts with which Methuen is currently flooding the market'). But more commonly it chose to present itself as a concern for the intellectual and moral well-being of 'students'. 'University students who come out of school with less and less confidence in their own ability to nose out the good from the bad, the genuine from the meretricious, are easy victims.' 'All over the country students are now being victimized by this attitude to literary studies.' 'Orthodoxy is also increasingly evident in the formal content of higher education courses and, more insidiously but coercively, in the more or less subtle censorship of oral and written discourse in the academy.' The charge of censorship is particularly poignant, given the frequency and fervour with which the champions of discrimination called for the liquidation of the book, the series, the publisher and everything in their vicinity. Even Claude Rawson, who watches his students cavorting in the theoretical playground with the tolerant avuncular twinkle of one who understands 'young people', reaches for his black cap when he turns to the publishers, and the General Editor, of the New Accents series:

> That these persons are in a position to exercise daily influence on an intellectually malleable section of the community is less disquieting than it might be: the young are open to ideas, good and bad, but they quickly acquire immunity to the galloping dottinesses of their elders . . . One may wonder at the process (blinkered impercipience? or cynical lucidity?) which got this book passed for publication by a reputable house.

What is going on here? How is it possible for a group of people, every one of whom would unhesitatingly endorse the arguments of Milton's *Areopagitica* and the aims of Amnesty International, to call without any consciousness of contradiction for the abolition of dissident books and courses and, by implication, of the people who write and teach them? One answer can be suggested by reflecting on the implications of key terms in the neo-traditionalist vocabulary: rigour, discrimination, selectivity. But beneath the offical discourse run the fault-lines of a deeper crisis. For there *is* a crisis in English—not so much in the subject itself, which never existed anyway outside the institutional relations and ideological conditions that constitute it, but in the self-valuation and identity of its *teachers*. Beleaguered on every side by a vindictive government, an indifferent public, ungrateful students, sceptical colleagues in the 'harder' faculties, small wonder if their inherited role as custodians of the national culture has come to feel a threatened and unvalued thing. Hence the consolatory incantation of talismanic formulae, the despairing invocation of 'absolute values' and 'traditional critical approaches', above all the rhetorical deployment of 'students', represented always as passive *victims*, mute, trusting, vulnerable. Of course it is vital, if this discursive strategy is to have its effect, that the 'silent majority of students' should never attempt to speak for themselves.

Notes

[1] *Re-Reading English*, ed. Peter Widdowson (London, 1982).

[2] *Times Literary Supplement*, 1 January 1982.

[3] *Times Literary Supplement*, 10 June 1983.

[4] *London Review of Books*, Vol. 4, No. 11

[5] *British Book News*, August 1982, p. 504.

[6] *Times Literary Supplement*, 10 December 1982.

[7] *London Review of Books*, Vol. 4, No. 24

[8] *PN Review* 40, p. 4.

[9] *PN Review* 40, p. 5.

[10] *PN Review* 42, p. 6.

[11] *PN Review* 30.

[12] *PN Review* 48, p. 5.

[13] John Milton, 'Of Education' (1644), in *Selected Prose*, ed. M. W. Wallace (Oxford, 1925).

Fear of the Happy Ending: 'The Color Purple', Reading and Racism

ALISON LIGHT

One of the many emotions I felt after reading this book was shame. Before I had forgotten or put aside my obligations as a woman, most of all as a black woman. Being wrapped up in myself I had forgotten the shit my sisters had to live through and even die for to put me where I am today: a Black woman able to think for myself, work for myself and plan my future.

(Review of *The Color Purple*, Gerry, *Spare Rib*, No. 135, October 1983).

Novels which change lives

This piece grows out of an earlier contribution to a collective presentation entitled, 'Problems of the Progressive Text' given at the sixth Literature/Teaching/Politics conference in 1985.[1] As lecturers in higher education we had chosen to discuss the specific delights and demands of teaching or studying those texts which appear to be overtly aligned with a left-wing politics, or whose radical reputation has gone before them, as it were. Alice Walker's *The Color Purple* (1982) seemed a good route into some of these issues since it ties together the major strands of a politics of difference—those of race, class and gender—in a contemporary bestseller by a black American feminist. Walker's story is the first-person narrative of Celie, a poor black girl in the Deep South between the wars; she relates, in a series of letters, the process of her eventual triumph over the most brutal forms of exploitation, her gradual recovery of her racial past and, via lesbianism, her claiming of an affirmatory sexuality. The novel, published here by The Women's Press, took the feminist world by storm even before it won the Pulitzer Prize in 1983. It has now been filmed by the Hollywood director, Steven Spielberg (he of *Jaws* and *E.T.* fame).

This tremendous take-off of a 'minority' text, however, not only highlights the problems of black writers being lionized by the dominant white culture; it raises also some crucial questions about the reading and reception of black writing by those of us, who, as white teachers and students, place or find such texts on the syllabus of 'English'. On the Left there has long been a deep and resourceful vein of 'countercriticism', criticism which reads 'classic' texts, the literary canon, against the grain, pointing up their complicity with dominant ideas and values and their refusal, however tortured, to admit the full range of cultural and social difference. Thus to teach a text like Walker's which speaks to and from those who are normally *absent* from the literary heritage of English, marginalized or oppressed groups, and in particular black women, sets us a different pedagogic and political agenda. *The Color Purple* is more about good subjects than bad objects; it closes with achievement and happiness, harmony and celebration—not topics which are easily accommodated by those left analyzes whose emphasis is finally upon struggle, strife and conflict.

In fact my own piece began from just such a nagging doubt about the pleasure of the text. How do we—as teachers—analyze a text which so many feminists, including myself, have felt to be about ourselves in powerfully involving and politicizing ways? Being on the side of the angels, such a novel brings forcefully home the fraught question of the influence and effect(ivity) of 'literature'. Do novels change lives, and if so, what (if any) is the job of criticism in relation to such experiences? How can the processes which the individual undergoes in reading be understood as part of that wider, collective struggle called politics? Further, what is the place of the pleasures of such a text—identification, affirmation, celebration—in political discourse and engagement?

These are some of the questions which I want to pursue here. To ask what goes on in the gap between reading and action is one way of trying to connect a cultural studies with a cultural politics, with what goes on *outside* the classroom. It is to refuse to polarize either 'culture' or 'politics' in a familiar opposition which designates the one as purely academic or aesthetic, and the other as divorced from the making of representations and their reception.[2] Instead we need to ask how the structuring of pleasures and anxieties in the practices of reading and writing help to maintain or disrupt our notions of our 'selves' in those other modes of our existence; what kinds of subjectivities are formed and offered by different texts and what are the political parameters and perimeters of our readings: what do they mean for different groups at different times in history and the culture?

Such questions take on an especially urgent form in relation to black culture when we ask them as white people in the 1980s. For how are we to understand our own 'identification' and solidarity whilst still acknowledging the political reality of difference? What indeed are we doing as white readers and white teachers when we read the black text? How are the meanings of our readings to be situated within an understanding of the history and formation of racial subjectivities? And how far do the writing and reading practices of what is revealingly called 'English' shore up and reproduce precisely, Englishness, a sense of cultural difference which depends in part on a notion of racial superiority and a history of imperial power?

The pleasures of reading and the power of racism, the connections between our supposedly private fantasies and our so-called public politics—this is an enormous area, and I shall do little more than skate across its surface. As was made clear by black delegates at the LTP conference, it is our own ignorance as white academics which has made for some pretty thin ice in places. Yet ironically, it is the passionate hopefulness of a text like *The Color Purple* which may at least help us to get our skates on. For Alice Walker's novel remains for me a profoundly inspiring and contradictory text because it is finally *utopian*: it is a fantastic success story, offering its readers an imaginary resolution of political and personal conflicts. It is the meanings and difficulties of this utopianism, how it might direct our readings and mobilize us politically, which I want to explore further.

Problems of identification

> You got to fight. You got to fight. But I don't know how to fight. All I know how to do is stay alive.[3]

I co-taught *The Color Purple* recently on an adult education course, a group of about ten women, all white and mostly under thirty, although one woman was in her sixties, and of whom about half were graduates. After reading short stories (Kate Chopin, Katherine Mansfield) and extracts on 'women and writing' we chose *The Color Purple* as the only complete novel read, in the hopes that it would bring together our earlier discussions of race, class and sexual politics. Importantly, and perhaps typically, we were not looking at the text in the context of other black writing, nor even of American literature, but in the context of contemporary feminism. Nevertheless as tutors we were surprised that the discussion did not lead into the issue of racism, and at the ways in which it did not.

Our readings began instead from a position of identification rather than of difference. Many students, like myself, had found the novel deeply moving on first reading, and had been exhilarated by its ending. The opening passages of Celie's brutal treatment, in which she, as teller of her tale, is never ultimately left degraded or without dignity, and her finding of sexual pleasure or social peace—we all talked about the power and appeal of such writing in terms of recognizing, identifying with, and desiring such affirmation as women, white, working-class, middle-class, feminist or no. We felt strongly drawn into the novel because of its structure of Celie's articulation of her life. Yet it was staggering how quickly the discussion became negative when we began to 'criticize'. The shift from re-telling the pleasure of reading to analyzing its meanings was severe and dramatic. I noted down at the time that 'the book threw up the issues of its language and of Celie's development—who it was for—and of its possible romanticism. I felt people were being very heavy about the happy ending, as though it were necessarily a bad thing'.

I am still intrigued by that last comment—'as though it were *necessarily* a bad thing'. Why were we so afraid of the happy ending and what does it mean for a group of white students to see as 'romantic' the empowering of an impoverished, beaten, raped and abused Southern black woman? Ironically, whilst we were involved in the novel's project as women, our critical terms for theorizing the questions of social and sexual conflict in a woman's life seemed to lead us into a disavowal of the importance of that process. We could only describe Celie's enrichment in a series of negative -isms: romanticism, idealism, sentimentalism, all smacked of dismissiveness. It seemed that as feminists we could never be satisfied with being satisfied; the novel's appeal to the possibility of an achievable, social and sexual transformation of your life seemed both deeply pleasurable and deeply suspect.

There were several issues at stake in this disjuncture. It might be that the problem was simply one of reading, of the strategies of English which brought with it an emphasis upon character and moral growth ('Celie's development'), and through whose distorting lens we had read the story and re-focussed it as an image of self-fulfilment and liberal humanist values, without realizing our own short-sightedness. This slippage from pleasure to displeasure could be seen as a function of English and/or Englishness—a refusal to engage with difference, all those discourses which make the text quite 'foreign' to our own culture. Alternatively, there seemed to be a special problem with the structure of the text itself, its first-person narrative which invited the mechanism of identification and needed it in order to be read. In both cases we are brought up against the complex question of politicization, either proceeding from the unifying claim to solidarity or from the fictional process of identifying, which leads us to wonder what part the formation of such 'identities' as woman, or black woman, might play in the generation of, and involvement with, any political discourse.

Is it English?

> The real question, however, it appears to me, is not whether poor people will adopt the middle-class mentality once they are well fed; rather, it is whether they will ever be well fed enough to be able to choose whatever mentality they think will suit them.[4]

Critics of the text, including some of my colleagues in the LTP presentation, have pointed out various reasons why *The Color Purple* is particularly vulnerable to the ravages of English. Unlike elsewhere in her work (in *Meridian* for example), Walker is not primarily concerned here with black struggle against white racism but with experience within the black community, within families and sexual relationships. This foregrounding of 'the private sphere' has made it possible for the question of difference, racial, sexual, social, to be ignored and effaced as a conflictual and political force and to be reformulated in the rhetoric of a liberal humanism (of which English is one discourse) as a repository of essential and eternal truths about a universal human condition. Celie's story in such a reading becomes a kind of latter-day 'Bildungsroman', her coming to power an embourgeoisment accompanied by the necessary modicums of moral wisdom and self-knowledge. Thus *The Washington Post*, heading the British edition, can call Walker's novel 'a fable for the modern world', reducing or transforming into myth the actuality of the social historical conditions and ideologies round which the text is constituted. Universalizing the specificity of the tale (the words 'black' and 'lesbian' do not appear on the cover of the The Women's Press edition), reproducing an invisibility to which those who are defined as 'other' are consigned by the dominant culture, such homogenizing makes the text more manageable, more marketable. Difference which is potentially alienating, frightening and challenging, is written out in favour of a transhistorical truism: as the advertising trailer for the film puts it, 'It's about life. It's about love. It's about us.'

Recent critical theories, notably within marxism and feminism have made the exposure of this rhetoric of liberal humanism a prime target, and have revealed the ideological positions which have lurked beneath the appeal to equality, liberty and fraternity (sic). The claim of the white bourgeois male to full subjecthood has often depended historically and socially upon the relegation and exclusion of all others from just this status: the dark continent, the great unwashed, the second sex, all these others are pushed to the margins of humanity, sometimes, as in the racist theories of the nineteenth century, even denied such humanity.

But these naturalizations of the political in favour of the eternal drama of the humanist self are not the only potentially racist response. Ironically, those of us for whom this critique appears a political priority can be as much dominated by liberal humanism in our rejection of its terms as in any complicity with them. To reduce Walker's text to these discourses in order to 'criticize' it—a reading, which as white educated subjects we can well afford—is equally a way of holding on to a cultural supremacy, of denying and incorporating difference: an attempt at colonization. My own first reading, for example, saw Walker's visionary ending as akin to 'the synthetic and religiose American familialism of *The Waltons*'.[5] This cheap joke (which got me a laugh at the conference) betrays not just my own ignorance but a complicated travesty both of the actual history of white Americans (as opposed to the normative and conservative marketing of it on T.V.), and of the very different relation which black familialism has had to capitalism given the history of slavery and of racism itself, especially in the South. Similarly, (mis)reading the question of spirituality in the novel, wearing the cultural blinkers of English Protestantism, is to be equally ideologically blinded by our own cultural discourses; such misrecognitions can easily slide into a refusal to accept the very different meanings and possibilities which 'religion' has had for black struggle.[6]

English, then, moves in mysterious ways. At its most obvious it shores up the racist response of one student who literally could not read the text because its language was 'primitive', 'badly written': it simply wasn't English, in all senses of the word. More tricky is the colonization of the text via the naturalizing aesthetic of lit. crit. which collapses its cultural specificity into moral value, emptied of any social or political referent: a 'consummately well written novel' enthused the *New York Times Book Review*, whilst the US *Tribune* praised its 'sweetness of tone . . . the sweep and daring of its literary ambition'.[7] Both responses efface the material and political conditions within which black language emerged as a *weapon* against, as well as a consequence of, slavery, and as a means of creating and maintaining a separate and inviolable community for black people in the face of white oppression.[8] Yet those of us who reject the interpretation of Celie's story as yet another journey into bourgeois bliss must find ways of affirming black power and achievement; we can hardly want only fictions in which black protagonists remain powerless—we have had those for centuries. For without such acknowledgment a familiar double-bind operates whereby the black subject is robbed of history and status either by being incorporated and ignored by the dominant social order or by being made visible *only* as victim, a helpless sufferer condemned to pain. Whether difference is therefore denied altogether, or whether it is (often simultaneously) insisted upon only as lack and failure, both strategies work to subordinate black people. This has long been part of our English inheritance, though such strategies have taken on new historical forms since the war in our dealings with 'decolonialization'.[9] *The Color Purple* is vividly at odds with the myth that 'freedom and whiteness [are] the same destination'.[10]

Clearly, for white academics, part of the problem is that *The Color Purple* is not about 'us' at all. Nothing is harder than for those who trade in knowledge to admit ignorance. What is even more threatening is to feel that those outside of 'our' dominant culture do have a knowledge and strength of their own precisely *because* of being outside. Not only is it often the case that only those who take privilege and comfort for granted are able to be dismissive about the struggle to leave poverty and hardship behind; it is also such people who are unable to learn that different lives produce their own equally important forms of knowledge and community—knowledge, from which they are by definition excluded. Wanting *The Color Purple* (as I did) to lead into a discussion of racism is certainly easier than seeing myself as marginal to its concerns. Thus any real engagement with racial difference in the text (and in our politics) has to be far more dialectical than any simple model of 'otherness' and its recuperation or appropriation (embourgeoisment) within the dominant culture, might propose. It means in part giving up the power of naming and of assuming knowledge of someone else's struggle, accepting that there are things which we cannot share, and intitiatives which we cannot create. Otherwise, as Stuart Hall and Martin Jacques have argued

> our model of society is that the only things worth getting involved with are our things; others are not capable of creating movements and currents which deserve our support, enthusiasm and intervention. This is a very patronizing view of the world.[11]

And when white readers refuse to listen to the black voice, accusing it instead of some kind of ventriloquism, such patronization is deeply racist.

There are many inroads to be made still into the territory of 'English', ways of fragmenting that impulse to homogenize and thereby control the diverse subjects and subjectivities which come within its boundaries. Cora Kaplan has pointed to some of the strategies of re-education which the white British reader might need in order to situate *The Color Purple* more properly in the historical, social and textual relations from which it emerged.[12] But for this process to be anything more than a textual encounter of the academic kind, we have also to press hard upon our first 'naïve' readings which will tell us more about our own relation to difference, the assumptions with which we start and which structure our pleasures and anxieties as white readers. We need to return to our 'selves' not in order to wallow in guilt but because such selves are historically and socially produced. In doing so, however, it is clear that deconstructing 'English' is only part of the story since, as my own course insisted, no text can be read or written solely as addressing one form of difference; the structures of racial, sexual and class difference intersect and often contradict each other, offering a range of positions to the reader, never simply a unitary or unified one. It is to the positive possibility of these identifications which do not deny difference, but work in tandem with them, that I want now to return.

The politics of utopianism

> I'm so happy, I got love, I got work, I got money, friends and time.[13]

I have argued that *The Color Purple* appeals especially to readers of *all* kinds because it is utopian in its form: Celie gets it all at the end of the story, and through her we are offered this dream of full achievement, of a world in which all conflicts and contradictions are resolved. Whilst I have maintained that such fictions *mean* very differently for different groups in the culture, nevertheless there is a bottom level at which *The Color Purple* keys into a far more diffuse desire for personal and social changes, what Carolyn Steedman has called 'historically much older articulations—the subjective and political expressions of radicalism'.[14] The desires for a world in which all people might have love, work, friends, money and time, underpin political theories like socialism and feminism: an appeal to the possibility of amelioration, of 'progress', which is no less potent or mobilizing for being an imaginary vision, a happy ending still to come.

Yet it is the power and persuasiveness of these desires which the Left has so frequently found problematic, from the debates around Owenite socialism to the politics of the peace movement.[15] Part of the response—that fear of the happy ending—has been a definition of radical politics which sees itself as one half of a binary opposition (left as opposed to right), and conceives its job as one solely of critique from underneath the dominant culture, as it were. In this definition the day of *not* having to be on the left never comes. This structural definition, however, offers little or insufficient insight into why people join and remain within political struggles, unless one assumes a rampant or global masochism. At its worst such a position becomes a moralistic kill-joyism which finds all pleasures in political engagement guilty ones, and indeed can see the question of pleasure itself as ideologically unsound. Running through such uneasiness is ironically a strong thread of empiricism, an insistence on the world 'out there' as separable and separate from the world 'in there' and a one-way model of determination. Such a model insists upon a divisive opposition which wrenches apart the field of 'the political' from that of personal or subjective space. The recalcitrant psyche, thus nominated, cannot then keep up with the revolutionary political/public Joneses and must be dismissed or denigrated, either as outside of social or cultural change and determined by that 'outside', or as irredeemably interior—'confessional', 'sentimental', 'romantic', 'private', 'personal'—depending on your century. Feminism alone, in its long dialogue with socialist theory, has pointed to the androcentricity implicit and produced in the making of these spheres. For clearly such demarcations of knowledge and power have political effects, working through and speaking through, for example, the meanings given to sexual difference.

Thus a novel such as *The Color Purple* can be popular with a whole range of women readers, cutting across the specificity of its black history, in its concern with family, emotionality, sexual relations and fantasy life. Walker herself has noted the operation of such collusive divisions of psychic and social existence in reproducing the inequalities of gender *and* race:

> black writing has suffered because even black critics have assumed that a book that deals with the relationships between members of a black family—or between a man and a woman—is less important than one that has white people as primary antagonists. The consequence of this is that many of our books by 'major' writers (always male) tell us little about the culture, history, or future, imagination, fantasies, and so on, of black people, and a lot about isolated (often improbable) or limited encounters with a non-specific white world.[16]

What is crucial in our understanding of the 'utopian' appeal of the text is not to reinstate subjectivity at the expense of 'the social' but to begin to dissolve those polarities, seeing the structures and site of subjectivity as exactly (equally) social and historical, equally the site of the operations of power. Terms like 'sentimental' and 'idealistic' are not themselves transparent descriptions of knowledge or response. They carry with them cultural prescriptions and assumptions and have themselves to be historicized. Not coincidentally both women's and black writing have been accused of 'emotionalism'. We need to ask why this *is* an accusation. Who is calling whom sentimental, when, and with what effect?

So to call *The Color Purple* 'utopian' is the beginning of an analysis, not the end of it. Words like this signal the insistent presence of the demands of subjectivity—of how sexual and racial differences come to be lived and felt in the act of living—as being a pressure in excess of what is 'realistically' on offer in a culture. Fiction, like fantasy, is the place of this excess. It re-informs and re-imagines the scene of its production, the unconscious as well as conscious desires which social relations cannot or will not fulfil. In other words, these questions of the 'effects' of reading, of the mobilizing of desires and pleasures in the activity of reading, are questions about fictionality itself; the processes of reading and writing occupy *simultaneously* intimate and public (because linguistic) space, space where desire and history intersect in the subjects of those practices (writers, readers, 'characters') and where new subjectivities can be formed. Such subjectivities are shown to be constantly negotiated, constantly fragmented and contradicted by the differences (racial, sexual, class-based) which they simultaneously try to unify and encompass. These 'identities' are broken up as soon as they are forged, seeming only to remain stable at the novel's point of closure—the happy ending—but this is the point at which the disjuncture between 'fiction' and 'life' is most apparent, where you shut the book and go off to face another fragmenting day.

All fictions are utopian—though some more than others; the worry about how politically mobilizing fiction can be is a worry about the tension within the act of representation itself. Subjects, in texts as in life, are constituted and re-constituted around those cultural interpretations of, or meanings given to, difference, which always threaten to disrupt the security of defining one 'self' solely or fully as, for example, a woman, a black person. Literary texts, and pre-eminently novels, take subjectivity as their material, but to argue that any reader is either fully positioned by a novel or can ever fully resist its strategies is to underestimate the contradictory process at the heart of linguistic representation: a process in which subjects, even as they gesture toward that idealized and coherent 'I' who will be marvellously coping, miraculously loving and loved, run headlong into the de-stabilizing actuality of what it means to be 'woman', 'black', 'poor' and so on, in the world.

If *The Color Purple* allows readers to speak their rage or their delight because of its appeal to a unified self, that appeal is precisely fictional, or fictitious, appealing because there is not and cannot be—other than in fictions—a safe and sealed place in which to find or be such a self. This self can be recognized both as an effect of language and of the attempt to heal the split demanded in the act of representation. It has also to be acknowledged, nevertheless, as a fiction which keeps us sane and active. For without such momentary fixings of the flux of subjectivity, the illusion of being a powerful and coherent agent in the world, how would we get out there and do things—how indeed can we have a political theory of action and responsibility? If we do not accept the force and temporary necessity of such identifications, textually and socially, are we not condemned to a theory of being which leaves us stranded in a quicksand of discursivity, fascinated but finally immobilized by 'the play of difference', fragmented always and totally, unable not just to act politically (to see and know ourselves collectively), but to act at all?

Perhaps it is not that we need to act as though we believe utopian achievements are possible—that like Celie we really will get it all; rather it seems that we need to believe in such utopias in order to act, in order to survive as human beings, making our own texts and histories in the face of the divisions and conflicts in our psychic/social existences which determine and fragment us. As Juliet Mitchell has written,

> We all live within ideology, both the general ideology of all human society and the specific ideologies of our times. It may well be the case that the humanist ideology is in itself only the liberal side of the capitalistic, free-enterprise coin—but we cannot escape it: must live ourselves (indeed, be ourselves) within its meanings while we are in such a society.[17]

To ignore the power of the fictional 'I', however much it is a figment of humanist ideology, is to risk denying the need which we have to believe that we are at the centre of our lives, a motivating need felt strongly too by those who have been oppressed by, and want to challenge the forms of this society. It is to risk robbing subjects of the chance to construct alternative histories of the world and of its power-relations, and of their politicizing visions of the future—however much we must insist on the ultimate fictionality of these accounts. For where would political struggle against oppression, against misery, be without such human narratives? The narratives may be inventions, but the suffering people cause one another, and the pleasure they are capable of giving each other, exist and continue to exist.

Unhappy ending?

> It is the misfortune (but also perhaps the voluptuous pleasure) of language not to be able to authenticate itself . . . language is, by nature, fictional.[18]

Fictions are fickle and cannot alone guarantee the political directions which our identifications might take. Reading the black text as a white reader, even as a feminist or a socialist reader, does not guarantee reading as an anti-racist. On the other hand, in terms of teaching and of political solidarity there will also be readers who strongly object to having what is the moment of their politicization 'de-constructed'. The problem is how not to undermine the strategic importance of that solidarity—wherever it appears—whilst remaining open to difference, critical of any final fixing of the meanings and forms of the political. Texts like *The Color Purple* are important because they signal the tension between the necessary rhetoric of desire for identification, the importance of the imaginary unified subjectivity in the process of politicization—the tension between *that* enabling dream and the forms which such 'selves' might take in our daily lives. For fixings can all too easily become fixed, a refusal of difference and a re-instatement of new but equally authoritarian power-structures. Such absolutism is a danger for any politics. Identifying ourselves as 'woman', 'black', 'working-class' can only be staging-posts on the 'road to revolution'; they cannot be places where we want to settle indefinitely. Neither the process of politicization nor that of social change can be so simply or reassuringly 'progressive'. Stable moments of solidarity may give us the energy to move on but it is the tension between solidarity and difference which creates political urgency, and it is the dialectical relation between our knowledge and our ignorance of others which keeps a political movement moving.

Finally then, for white academics, challenging English means inevitably untacking the subjectivities in which we have dressed our selves for a long time. Many of us have indeed been made by books. It hurts to discover that so many of our investments—literally economic, as well as social and personal—are going bankrupt. For women like myself, who made the move from the working classes via a 'liberal arts' education, it is intensely painful, as well as hard, to continue to attack the positions which have only just conceded me a foothold in the dominant culture. I suspect, however, that if we cannot give up that power and those securities peaceably and in co-operation, then we will lose them in any case on much stonier ground in future struggles, when solidarity and difference will be posed as exclusive alternatives, and black and white a violently polarized opposition.

So when as critics we warn against the essentializing tendencies of humanist fictions, we need nevertheless to recognize their democratizing potential, their celebration of human agency and activity—an impulse without which both socialism and feminism are inert. Not to do that, and to dismiss the powerful optimism and the collective historical significance of a text like *The Color Purple* is to throw out the baby with the bathwater. Which is not just anti-humanist, but inhumane.

Notes

[1] LTP is a national network of teachers and students who hold an annual conference and produce a journal. The 1985 papers are available (£1.25) from Helen Taylor, Department of Humanities, Bristol Polytechnic. I would like to thank the other members of the Sussex group, and especially Rachel Bowlby, for their help with this piece.

[2] See Janet Batsleer *et al.*, 'Culture and politics', in *Rewriting English* (London, 1985).

[3] *The Color Purple*, (London, 1983), p. 17.

[4] Alice Walker, *In Search of Our Mother's Gardens* (London, 1984), p. 126.

[5] *LTP Conference Papers* (Bristol, 1985), p. 130.

[6] See, for example, Alan Sinfield's discussion in the LTP 1985 papers; and Cedric J. Robinson's *Black Marxism: The Making of the Black Radical Tradition* (London, 1983).

[7] Quoted on the back cover of The Women's Press 1983 edition.

[8] See B. Bryan, S. Dadzie and S. Scafe, *The Heart of the Race: Black Women's Lives in Britain* (London, 1985), especially Chapter 5.

[9] See Centre for Contemporary Cultural Studies analysis, *The Empire Strikes Back: Race and Racism in 70s Britain* (London, 1982).

[10] Walker, *In Search*, p. 291.

[11] 'People Aid', *Marxism Today*, July 1986.

[12] 'Keeping the Color in *The Color Purple* (LTP Bristol 1985); see also, for further reading, the debates in *Feminist Review* no. 17 (1984), no. 20 (1985) and no. 23 (1986)

[13] *The Color Purple*, p. 183.

[14] *Landscape For a Good Woman* (London, 1986), p. 14.

[15] See, for example, Barbara Taylor, *Eve and The New Jerusalem: Socialism and Feminism in the Nineteenth Century* (London, 1983).

[16] Walker, *In Search*, p. 261.
[17] *Women: The Longest Revolution* (London, 1984), p. 247.
[18] Roland Barthes, *Camera Lucida* (London, 1984), p. 85.

English Teaching and Media Education: Culture and the Curriculum

DAVID LUSTED

One of the historic peculiarities of the British education system has been its resistance to changing a curriculum still significantly located in the state of late nineteenth-century knowledge. The secondary school timetable, in its particular combination of separate *subjects* of study, is the archetypal relic of this earlier order. And this is so, notwithstanding the various accommodations that have taken place over time resulting from attempts to modernize the curriculum through the introduction of additional subjects. Although, on the surface, the curriculum looks like a veritable Babel of voices, at its core it has long been univocal.

It would be irony indeed, then, if this pattern were at last to be broken as an unintended consequence of the current government's regressive attempts to re-establish firmer boundaries between the academic and the vocational, between education and training. Signs are, however, that quite surprising curriculum interventions are at work in the body education, a posse of Trojan horses containing forces quite at odds with the instrumental intentions behind recent initiatives such as those leading to examination reorganization at 16+ and the establishment of the Technical and Vocational Education Initiative (TVEI) at secondary level.

One of the most significant of these new forces for English teaching in particular and the curriculum in general lies in movements rethinking, yet again, the relations between art and society, culture and language. New directions in literary theory and media sociology combine with debate over new technologies and changing leisure patterns to produce a new educational consciousness of the importance and complexity of the terms in these relations. For many years, English teachers have recognized the need to study areas of cultural production other than the literary—advertising and newspaper journalism, for instance. And the curriculum has traditionally, if marginally, noted the language of the audio-visual image as well as the written and spoken word. Contemporary movements share the spirit of such developments, yet promise more extensive and more holistic approaches. Such approaches are signalled by developing terms like 'media education' in the 5–16 curriculum, 'media studies' at 16+, and 'cultural studies' in higher education.

It is important to avoid claiming too much for these terms. Individually, they are no more than emergent educational movements. Collectively, they do not, as yet, represent an integrated disciplinary programme for different sectors of education. Rather, each bears its own specific history, carries different inflections and tensions, addresses different combinations of study objects. Nonetheless, they bear sufficient similarities, not least in sharing a commitment to a realignment of interest around what has been conventionally termed 'the humanities', to justify thinking of them as constituents of a new educational movement, the one that provides my focus here.

As far as curriculum matters are concerned, 'media education' functions as a useful generic title for this new movement. It implies more inclusive approaches to *language* and *culture* through a complex notion of *media*. This term has to bear a great deal of meaning, so it is worth spending time specifying its range of connotations.

First, there is the sense of media as the *raw materials* of cultural production; pens and paper, 'fine art' materials most obviously, but also the technologies related to them like typewriters and printing presses. By extension, we must go on to include technologically-based materials like film and video. The whole implies an extension of learners' own practices, across a wide range of media and beyond the familiar categories of writing and speaking, to provide the widest possible range of experience of 'speaking', making meaning, through the widest available media means.

Second, raw materials, once worked on, are made into *products* in any one of a variety of forms. Various literary forms find counterparts in other media, sharing especially generic similarities as in the melodrama or the gothic romance, and they also bear distinctive individual qualities; although the novel, the narrative feature film and the television serial share many formal traits, the way in which each is experienced, its conditions of reception or consumption, makes for a very different relation between 'text' and 'reader'. A similar argument can be made for non-fiction forms, in studying relations across and between the production of news in newspapers and television news programmes, for instance.

What is at stake in making these combinations for study is not least in forcing a greater connection between learners' own production and that offered by the leading media institutions—the publishing houses, the broadcast companies, the film industry, etc. Forms already exist in which media products dominantly take shape. All of us, at least to some extent, take models for our own production from those available around us and no teacher will need reminding of the tensions between these models and the conditions in which we can produce in the classroom, where the resources, time and skills available to us are limited. There are significant differences, then, in what can be produced through the dominant practices of media organizations and the subordinate practices of sites outside the mainstream. A focus on a wide range of media products for study, therefore, also includes concern with the *processes* through which products come to be.

As a simple case study to exemplify these ideas, take the *family snapshot album*. Although many of us take photographs, most are produced within the form of snapshots, rather than portraits, photojournalism or art-photography. Some snapshots display more skill than others, for sure, but it takes very little study to discern a set of conventions, 'ideals in our heads', which govern the process and production of snapshots for all of us. Studying our own production of snapshots in relation to the institution of the family album *historicizes* and *socializes* our understanding. Such a study connects our own production to that of the major media organizations, making both available for analysis.

Unsurprisingly now, the third notion of media calls up the media *institutions*, those organizations and agencies in the business of producing, distributing and exchanging media products on larger or smaller scales. The notion of institution refers to specific corporations—like the Mirror Group, the BBC and Goldcrest Films—as well as the larger media phenomena they exemplify—Fleet Street, the British broadcast network and Hollywood. In the same way that the social sciences extend the metaphor of the institution to include, say, the family or the monarchy, so the notion of the media institution includes such practices as journalism, 'showbusiness' and even archiving.

The inter-play of these three notions of (the) media has a particular explanatory power. It can account for a complex of cultural experience: in the relation between what learners produce themselves and have produced for them through the media institutions; in learners' roles not only as media producers but also as members of various 'audiences' for media products; in understanding interconnections between the media (in their financing, production deals and organization, local, national or global); in identifying changes across different cultures (how television in Britain is organized differently from television in Italy or Cuba, for instance); in identifying our differential access to the means of media production (almost anyone can take a snapshot but how many of us get to screen their video production on prime-time television?).

Importantly, this complex notion of media refuses any idea of the current state of media organization as inevitable. Instead it allows for demonstrations of change over time and the possibility of future change. In such a framework, the cultural status of the novel, for instance, can be grounded historically, the organization of broadcasting in Britain can be discerned as the product of political choices rather than in the nature of the medium itself. Perhaps most crucially, learners can come to see themselves as part of the object of study, part of a culture in which their own identities and subjectivities, their own choices, are at stake.

Notions of the media in media education, then, offer extensions to the conventional range of study objects in English teaching. But how does media education offer terms to rethink the nature of the investigation of this new alignment of study objects? The answer lies in further extensions of the notion of language and of the location of culture.

Customarily, English teaching divides language into two parts: as a *function of communication* and as *aesthetic expression*. The first is applied to a broad range of non-fictional forms, some vocational like records and memos, others in forms of reportage or testimony. The second is most often applied to a much narrower range of elite fiction—novels (for the most part realist), drama, poetry—beside which our own production appears inevitably meagre and mean. What media education draws attention to is the distinct ways in which each of these forms produces meaning, regardless of the value placed upon specific examples, and across the widest range of media artifacts. The visual image, the television game show, the cinema feature film—all produce rather than reflect meaning through a range of formal procedures and cultural references, in different but comparable ways to the novel or the government report. Analysis will be sensitive to formal and generic differences but ultimately the 'test' of meaning is located in *contexts*; how any given product is offered institutionally and how it is 'taken up' and used by its socially-positioned 'reader'.

For this mode of analysis, therefore, it would be insufficient to uncover the intentions of the author, Thomas Mann, or the politics of the publishers, Rupert Murdoch, and read off the meaning of *Death in Venice* or *The Sun* therefrom. Nor would it be adequate to analyze the linguistic structures and modes of expression of either of these, now, literary pieces in order to construct an ideal, better or worse read/informed reader. More, it becomes possible to seek out how this novel or this newspaper has the literary status or the mass appeal it enjoys through its institutional position; how it comes to be that a minority audience is 'called up' to appreciate the cultural status of the one and how a broad swathe of mainly working-class readers are 'called up' to daily purchase of the culturally-despised other.

As a classroom strategy, this mode of media education analysis has many attractions. It provides a productive space (rather than, as is often the case, a resisted one) in which learners can come into contact with forms of cultural production outside the experience of their class, race, gender and age. It enables comparative analysis of study objects within that range and in relation to more familiar cultural objects. And, most importantly, it values, though not necessarily uncritically, learners' own cultural choices and senses of self, enabling grounds for risking subjectivities in unthreatening but challenging ways and to productive, revealing effects.

This leads us to a new set of understandings of the term 'culture'. In media education, 'culture' is not rendered as coterminous with 'art', not at all as a range of (mainly elite) productions, nor as a catch-all 'society' (Raymond Williams's 'whole way of life'). Rather, 'culture' stands to include all cultural *production*, of whatever significance and whether conventionally understood formally as art, entertainment, information or education. It also refers to all cultural *relations*, whether entered into at a personal level or, more distantly, through the representations offered by the range of institutions around us. Cultural relations are identified in our domestic, work and leisure practices, our 'daily life', as well as in our understandings of others met only through their representation(s) in newspapers, party political leaflets, television programmes, poetry or whatever.

Further, this more extensive notion of culture is not something 'out there' that we dispassionately observe, to choose or reject. It is our sense of self, differentially-located in our social identities as men or women, black or white, of one class fragment or another, regionally-located, or as specific neighbours, lovers, workers and even, in the classroom, as teachers or learners. In the same way that language not only expresses what we choose to say, well or otherwise, but also *produces* us as members of specific social cross-groupings, so too are we produced *within* culture, cultures, and sub-cultures, more dominant in some than others, but for most, learners, especially, subordinated, less rather than more powerful, marginal rather than central. What media education offers, through its focus on cultural production and relations, is a greater understanding of social position, and terms for understanding alternatives in action for change. In classroom relations, the appeal lies not only in the access given to the widest range of cultural production but even more significantly in the attention it demands to specific social and cultural differences between and across learners and teacher, combining understanding in one shared cultural arena, accounting for meaning-differences in another, unshared. The pedagogy implied by media education is at once more open-ended, exploring terms of difference; and more explanatory, revealing the grounds of difference.

What is at stake here is much more than modernizing English teaching or expanding the subject of English. The existing organization of the curriculum actively inhibits the connections and revelations arising through the potential of media education through fragmenting its field of knowledge into different subjects, and valuing each differently. English, as a privileged subject, customarily separates language from literature, at worst instrumentalizing language acquisition, leaving skills of communication aside from the factors that control them, and reifying highly selective and evaluated texts as 'Literature' in a realm apart. This pattern is so tenacious, and the status of English so strong, that other subjects concerned with culture tend to be denied any interest in language. Art, for example, as a subject is left to celebrate individual expression and a bit of Art History at 16+ and beyond. Moreover, combined, these subjects in the curriculum colonize 'creativity' by connecting it to cultural production alone. Cultural relations are thereby left to educationists in those 'modern' subjects like Sociology and Geography which, in turn, lose much of their sense of history since it's dealt with in History lessons. Collectively these 'Humanities' subjects are split from the natural sciences, partially to align elsewhere in academic areas of the curriculum (mainly externally examinable!) where 'brainwork' is credited over 'training' which in turn is ascribed a lower status like 'practical work', in a classical mental/manual configuration of labour.

The present dominant organization of the curriculum makes 'culture' and 'language' inevitably instrumental terms; things to acquire, from 'out there', possessed by others to pass on to us, rather than things we learn about ourselves, from connections made between ourselves. The fragmentation of knowledge in the curriculum makes it almost impossible to make sense of our connections to a complex contemporary culture, to understand how *all* of us, rather than just an élite few, come to be as we are. The value-laden preoccupations of the curriculum also forces us to make continual judgements about forms of language and culture, and within that of ourselves also, without understanding either what's at stake in making those judgements or what forces lie actively behind their making.

In the past and under pressure, the reflex response to criticism of the curriculum, from every newly emerging position, has been to squeeze timetable space for additional subjects. The 'additive' principle has resulted in much hand-wringing over the 'overcrowded' timetable, coinciding however with popular demands for a return to a curriculum core. Clearly, calls for yet more additions to the subject-led curriculum are impossible.

Yet something has to be done to shake up the conventional curriculum. The 'classical disciplines' remain the dominant curriculum forces, certainly at least in the status ascribed to them, even though they are increasingly perceived as out of skew with the state of contemporary knowledge, cultural organization and even the (more suspect) 'demands of the economy'. Increasing numbers of learners, if proscribed by law from voting with their feet, appear to be voting with their heads: it's not necessary to subscribe to a conservative moral panic over the 'failure' of contemporary schooling in order to identify consumer resistance as evidence that the curriculum 'isn't working'.

If the curriculum is overcrowded it is precisely because of the failure to recognize that it is the constitution of the curriculum as a set of subjects that is at fault. What is required is more than additives or correctives to this structure. A substantial curriculum reorganization is required, perhaps along faculty lines, in debate over which emergent forces like media education will play a major part.

Much of this argument is in the realm of idealism, however, (though not 'impossibilism') and its rhetorical flourishes require more grounding in the current state of the politics of education. The curriculum of 'classical disciplines' has been under attack for some time and is currently under pressure from new initiatives mobilized by the state. The emergence of MSC schemes in secondary and further education, together with shifts in power from the DES and the LEAs to central government, exemplify the powerful pressures on the nature of the curriculum from directions quite other than those of the kind of explanatory and democratic movement identified here. It is worth taking space to account briefly for the recent history which underwrites the current state of politics in education.

The general education context is the break-up of a consensus view about the role and function of the education system, a consensus that held sway in the post-war period up until the early 1970s. During that time, debate took place over the *structure* of education, rather than its content. There was general agreement on the importance of education *for itself*; argument centred on the means to the widest access to education. The comprehensive school system developed from this commitment on the basis of arguments for equal access to education, 'equality of opportunity for all'.

A symbolic moment of change is marked by the speech of the then Prime Minister, James Callaghan, at Ruskin College in 1976 and the arising 'Great Debate' on education. The speech signalled an end to the all-Party consensus on education, shifting state priorities and resources elsewhere and forcing a closer relation between education provision and the assumed needs of the economy; in particular, changes in demand for labour in the job-market.

Since the late 1970s, this trend has developed apace through two terms of a conservative administration. Much of the argument of the initially-despised *Black Papers* at the turn of the 1970s has since become 'common-sense' in public exchange about education; assertions of 'declining standards', demands for 'accountability (sic) and efficiency', pressures for vocational training as a greater component of a general education, 'return to the three Rs', 'responding to the needs of industry', and so on. What motors this 'new consensus' is, of course, an economic argument: that (capitalist) market forces should determine not just the shape but also the *content* of education provision (although—in the planned incentives to spread private education provision, through direct grants and assisted places schemes, the laissez-faire policy on the education dispute and the continuing support of the Right for a form of 'voucher-scheme'— market forces still often seem to need a bit of a push from 'the nanny state').

Where the 'new consensus' *differs* from the previous one is in the understanding that the curriculum, the nature of the content of education, is as important a site for change as the more obvious structure of the education system. Contemporary central government initiatives arise from more than an intention to restructure education better to provide for newly hierarchized labour market. They are at the same time a programme for *cultural* change. The notion of the 'enterprise culture', well accounted for in Chancellor Lawson's 1986 budget speech, is nothing less than a thoroughgoing attempt to reconstruct consciousness of self as that of a prospective worker in 'national' and 'family' life, rather than as a member of groups in other social and cultural relations. These initiatives recognize how important it is to work for change, not just in institutions and arguments, but in people's heads, in their senses of life-expectations and social positions.

The object of the new initiatives in education is to obscure social difference and promote narrowly economic imperatives. State education is seen as the site where working-class learners especially are to be constructed in a less than active role in the 'new' enterprise culture; where they are to be trained in work practices (or, more likely, in a resignation to worklessness), and in disciplines better able to respond to the casualization of labour and the de-regulation of working conditions, among other demands set by the drivers of the enterprise. Meanwhile, a slightly modified set of 'classical disciplines' continue to be the route through an academic education for the pre-selected élite.

Although the *intentions* of these initiatives may be clear however, it would be premature to read off *effects* from them. The process of establishing the new initiatives carries risks. In opening up the question of the curriculum for the kinds of changes envisaged, quite contrary forces are enabled. This is true especially in the ways in which initiatives have sought to by-pass the professional education elites in favour of business management forces. The reduced power of the DES, and the reform of the Schools Council into the separate functions of curriculum development and assessment procedures was intended as a device to disenfranchise teacher representatives. Instead what has effectively happened is that the new managements have prescribed new course and examination *frameworks*, only to leave the content to quite new groups of educationists, often active and progressive classroom teachers, who have grasped the opportunity, together with the newly-available resources and constructed syllabuses, courses and modules, often with great imagination. Testimony of this lies in the quality of many of the new TVEI schemes and in the new GCSE and CPVE syllabuses at 16+ examination level.

It would be foolish to claim too much for these new forces; it is still early days and many of the challenging demands specified in the new course outlines have yet to be proved through classroom practice. Nonetheless, there is much documented evidence, at least, to indicate the promise of a small-scale revolution in curriculum design and practice. What is clear is that the curriculum of 'classical disciplines' is getting short shrift and many of the old holy writs are on the run. Assaulted in its core positions, under-resourced, contracting in timetable space, the old subject-centred curriculum looks to be in its twilight days.

My argument has been that this is little more than it deserves. The current education initiatives mobilized by the state provide opportunities to promote more forceful realignments in educational provision. Certainly, it is no cause for the chest-beating and nostalgic reveries characteristic of many of the traditional education lobbies.

The promise of 'media education', as one of a number of terms among the new movements, lies in a renewed impetus for claims to notions of culture and language to reappear, regenerated and with new powers of explanation, in a reorganized curriculum. The seeds lie, paradoxically, within the new initiatives, despite their aspirations to instrumentalize education.

The long-term objective for forces aspiring to a 'curriculum of today' is to work towards the foundation of a new Education Act under future administrations of more democratic tendencies than the present one. Under this Act, provision would be made for a structure that guarantees education over a lifetime, allowing for decision to opt out after a minimum mandatory period and the right to return at any time. Routes through this structure would tolerate the widest variety of courses fitted to the greatest expression of felt need, with forms of 'positive discrimination' to encourage access for those previously disenabled social groups of women, blacks, the very young and the very old, and the various factions within the old category of 'the working class'.

The curriculum would remain a general one but be reorganized to provide connections between arenas of knowledge and opportunities to specialize in certain disciplinary combinations, at any time. 'Language' and 'representation' would become key terms across teaching in all areas of a newly synthesized curriculum. Pedagogy would become critical rather than accommodative in its intent and practice. The purpose of education would be transformative rather than reproductive. Teachers and learners would be valued as cultural producers rather than merely as vectors of knowledge produced elsewhere. And the cultural sciences would take their place alongside the natural sciences as the major explanatory forces in an emancipatory late twentieth-century education system.

Enough dreaming. Yet much evidence of some such scenario for the future abounds at this time in the new curriculum movements currently at work in the education scene. Teachers (in the last analysis) and despite government policies which shift resources from education and aspire towards an instrumentalized curriculum, occupy the most strategic of positions. Whatever the governing conditions of the classroom, the relation between teacher and learner is where the real power lies to change consciousness. Through knowledge of this experience, teacher-led movements occupy a powerful position for curriculum change. My experience of many of those teachers active in the media education movement gives me some confidence in the possibility that, when education comes to seize *its* moment, new movements such as this will prove a powerful agency for change. English teachers have little to lose and much to gain from contributing to the new alignments.

Select Bibliography

Media Education Report (BFI, London, 1982)
Papers from the Bradford Media Education Conference (SEFT, London, 1986)
The English Department (ILEA English Centre, London, 1982)
John Ellis, *Visible Fictions* (London, 1982)
Richard Dyer et al., *Coronation Street* (London, 1981)
John Hartley, *Understanding the News* (London, 1982)
Nicholas Garnham and Joyce Epstein, *The State of the Art: or the Art of the State?* (GLC, London, 1985)
Catherine Belsey, *Critical Practice* (1980)
Pat Holland, 'The Page Three Girl Speaks to Women, Too', *Screen* 24, no. 3 (1983)
Raymond Williams, *Culture* (London, 1981)
Dick Hebdige, *Subculture: the Meaning of Style* (London, 1979)
CCCS Education Group, *Unpopular Education* (London, 1981)
Jo Spence, *Beyond the Family Album* (exhibition panels, on hire from Cockpit Cultural Studies Workshop, London) and *Putting Myself in the Picture* (Camden Press, 1987)

Notes on editors and contributors

Peter Brooker and Carolyn Brown are lecturers in English at Thames Polytechnic.

Tony Davies is a lecturer in English at Birmingham University.

Dee Edwards, David Maund and John Maynard have been teaching in various West Midlands colleges and schools for about ten years.

Michael Green is a lecturer in the Centre for Contemporary Cultural Studies at Birmingham University.

Paul Hoggart teaches English at Woolwich College in London.

Richard Hoggart was Professor of English at Birmingham and first Director of the Centre for Contemporary Cultural Studies there. He has later worked in UNESCO and been Warden of Goldsmiths' College, University of London.

Alison Light is a lecturer in English at Brighton Polytechnic.

David Lusted is an education adviser at the British Film Institute.

Michael Skovmand is a lecturer in English at the University of Aarhus.